WHEN SPIRITS SPEAK....

WE LISTEN

JOHN ZAFFIS

DEBBIE ELWARD

REVEREND LARRY ELWARD

ISBN: 9798491030576

DEDICATION

With over forty plus years of working within the paranormal field, we have had the privilege of encountering many different and unique paranormal enthusiasts. It is to those individuals we dedicate this book. You know what it is like to be on the paranormal front-line.

CONTENTS

INTRODUCTION

On the heels of their first book, What Lurks Within (which incidentally won first place in Paranormal Rewinds best paranormal book of 2020), John Zaffis, with Larry and Debbie Elward, have gotten together in a collaboration once again over their many, many years of working together in the business of trying to alleviate people of their problems that are associated with the paranormal. All three have a long -standing interest in the paranormal: John having grown up in a famous paranormal family; Larry, after watching the movie "The Exorcist" and wanting to be one; and Debbie having the gift of spirits, which is her ability to see, hear and feel spirits and wondering how to use them, and all three coming together with a common goal in helping people deal with their paranormal problems.

In this book, *When Spirits Speak...We Listen*, the three have once again reopened their case files and handpicked these cases in hopes of warning and teaching the readers as to the ways that demonic influence can intrude into one's life.

This book is a brutally honest non- fiction account of demonic intrusions into the lives of ordinary people...just like you and your next-door neighbor. It is an attempt to educate on the wiles and ways of the demonic. The three have attempted to explain as best they can the different aspects associated with an investigation of a haunting infestation, as well as other such manifestations in the supernatural.

There are many ghostly tales of spirit visitations into innocent people's lives. Read the true accounts about the ramifications of an entrepreneur's moving of a cemetery over a century ago, also of innocent children being enticed by demonic entities, and many more encounters of the demonic and hauntings by normal every-day people. Also included are the other worldly communications from loved ones from beyond the grave. This book is an attempt to explain the unexplained. So, turn on all the lights in your house and sit back and enjoy. And by the way...it is all true!

FOREWORD

"The Light shines in the darkness, and the darkness did not comprehend it." ~ John 1:5

Imagine a world filled with light and shadows.

The light represents all that is good: sunshine, the purity of unbridled love, the compassion one person has for another; while the shadows embrace all that is wicked and evil. One cannot exist without the other. Light is required to cast a shadow, but does not cast one itself. If the light weakens and fades, darkness has an opportunity to gain a foothold.

This is why we need the lightworkers – the bringers of goodness, the apostles of faith. They bravely charge into the darkest recesses, pushing the shadows away with the brightness of their being.

There are many variations of lightworkers. Some are medical professionals, pushing illness and injury away and replacing them with health and vitality. Others are simply normal people who see the world through rose colored glass, helping others to look for the good instead of focusing on the bad. And some are warriors.

Like most of you reading this, I first learned about John Zaffis on a paranormal television show. He was the demonologist brought in to help a family with an extreme haunting. Later, I saw him on *The Haunted Collector*, but I didn't truly appreciate him until I met him in person.

As a paranormal author, I was attending my very first paranormal convention in Salem, Massachusetts. At the time, I had five or six titles, and I had no idea how many books to bring. Would I sell five books or fifty? I didn't know, so I ordered more than I thought I'd need and carted them into the convention room. I sat at my booth for eight hours, only selling a few copies. As the event closed for the day, I needed to lug all those books back out to my car.

I borrowed a hotel luggage cart and stacked my big, heavy boxes on it, struggling to wheel it across the carpeted lobby. The boxes shifted and leaned with every push, but I made it all the way to the double doors. As I started through, one of the doors closed and knocked all my books off the luggage cart.

I nearly cried. Not only did I have an unsuccessful day with book sales, I now had to retrieve all the books that had spilled out of the boxes and onto the entry floor. People walked past me, stepping over my books. No one bothered to help me. As I attempted to collect my books, a man walked through the door and said, "Let me help you with that."

I looked up to see none other than John Zaffis. He knelt down on the floor and began helping me pick up my books. As others noticed him helping me, they too jumped in to assist. Soon the mess was cleared, and he walked me all the way to my car, even helping me lift the heavy boxes into the trunk of my car.

I'm not sure if John even remembers this, but it was a life altering moment for me. It made me truly appreciate the ability one person has to completely transform a moment, turning it from bad to good, dark to light.

The years passed, and I saw John at various paranormal conventions. I always found it remarkable just how humble and down-to-earth he was. I even commented to a friend, "Look at John Zaffis walking around as though he's not John Zaffis." And it was true. He was the one who talked to the shy people in the room who were too nervous to approach him. When he learned that I was writing a book about DeAnna Simpson's horrific haunting, one he had investigated, he approached me and asked me if I'd like him to write the foreword.

At some point during this, we became friends. We chatted on the phone and he introduced me to his friends Debbie and Larry Elward. When they penned a book together, they asked me if I would format it for them and help them get it published. Through this process I began garnering a better understanding of what these three people do. They are warriors.

Many of you probably know that John is a descendant of pure paranormal royalty. He learned most of what he knows at the elbows of his uncle and aunt, Ed and Lorraine Warren. He still brings Ed's old recorder with him on investigations and carries their words of wisdom everywhere he goes.

John continues their legacy along with the Elwards, helping others with their paranormal encounters. In many ways, the three of them are the dream team of the paranormal community. Debbie is a paranormal researcher and a psychic medium who is able to look beyond the veil and gain a better understanding of the haunting. Her husband, Larry, is an independent priest and exorcist, and John is a demonologist with four decades of experience.

What truly stuck with me after helping them publish their first book together, *What Lurks Within*, was how cohesive the three of them work together. They go into locations that others were unable to handle. They identify the haunting and then resolve it with love and compassion. They are the lightworkers, the warriors who push darkness away with light.

The world needs more of this. More of the light. Less of the dark. I'm grateful to know they are out there, making the world a better place. Every time they remove a negative entity, they claim more of the light. They will not let darkness gain a foothold on our realm, and I'm thankful for them.

Blessed are the lightworkers because they are the force that stands between us and the darkness.

Joni Mayhan

Joni Mayhan is a paranormal investigator and the author of 23 paranormal books, including Bones in the Basement – Surviving the S.K. Pierce Haunted Victorian Mansion and Hanover Haunting – The DeAnna

Simpson Story. To learn more about her, check out her website: Jonimayhan.com

GHOSTS, GHOSTS AND MORE GHOSTS

Photo by Dan LeRoy Productions, LLC | danleroyproductions.com

TYPES OF HAUNTINGS

It has been said, "Ghosts are not people...they are the unresolved emotions of people." Perhaps this explains why there are a lot of different types of hauntings and why in the forty plus years in paranormal work John, Debbie and Larry have personally witnessed just about all types of hauntings.

The first type of hauntings one may come across in the paranormal field is a "residual" haunting. This type is an energetic recording of an event that plays over and over; many times it is fueled by emotion, a date, or a location. According to Theosophist Alice A. Bailey, who writes in her book *Light of the Soul*, "The Akashic record is like an immense photographic film, registering all the desires and earth experiences of our planet. Those who perceive it will see pictured there on: The life experiences of every human being since time began, the experience of the entire animal kingdom, the aggregation of the thought forms of a karmic nature of every human unit throughout time. Here is the great deception of the records. Only a trained occultist can distinguish between actual experience and those astral pictures created by imagination and keen desire." There is no entity involved in this type of haunting so there cannot be any communication. This supernatural event can manifest in many ways such as apparitions, sounds.

Many times, a residual haunting is nothing more than sounds that are repeated... usually at the same time and location. Residual hauntings are many times located at a site like Gettysburg. One can only imagine the emotions of the gallant men fighting these battles on both sides. These emotions were strong enough to leave an impression on the "ether" or "Akashic" records in that area. This type of haunting is thought to be non-dangerous.

The next type of haunting is an "intelligent" haunting. This is where a spirit makes actual communication with a person or performs an act related to the location, or moves an object, such as opening and closing a drawer or a door. In this type of haunting the spirit is truly present. It has planned to stay in this world for some reason, whether it is an attachment to a person, place or thing. Many times, someone may have died unexpectedly and does not realize they have passed, or they may have unfinished business. Many times, these hauntings are tactile as well as physical...communicating, slamming doors or drawers, or other audible phenomenon. In other cases, they may manifest as an apparition or a ghost. Again, this type of haunting all though scary is not thought to me dangerous.

Next there is the "poltergeist" type of haunting. The term "poltergeist" comes from a German word meaning 'noisy ghost.' This is a haunting that is intense but short lived and usually centers around a specific person. There are many theories as to what the cause of poltergeist activity is, but many in the paranormal community believe it is caused by "psychokinesis," which is the ability to move items with the power of a person's mind. Poltergeist activity usually centers around children entering puberty. This is because of all the raging feelings and hormones that are commonly this time. While this can be a very destructive haunting, there is no religious answer or intervention that can be used in this type of haunting. It usually just ends by itself, for reasons to be determined. This type of haunting can be moderate in danger, depending on the spirit and the interaction.

The next type of haunting is a "shadow people" type of haunting. This is the most widely reported type of haunting. In this type of haunting, shadows are seen resembling a human form. These "shadow people" are seen as a fleeting glimpse from the peripheral vision, but once someone turns to see the movement, there is nothing there. Sometimes the "shadow person" is seen quite vividly and can be recorded in videos and photographs. Once again, all though scary, most shadow people type hauntings are not dangerous but also the interactions of people have to be taken into consideration.

The last type of haunting is, of course, the inhuman haunting, this involves an entity that was never human. It can make physical contact with objects and people with the sole purpose to disrupt lives and to possess and gradually mentally manipulate a person to do things that they would not normally do. This type of haunting is extremely dangerous and should only be attempted by seasoned paranormal investigators and experienced clergy.

Here are some cases of each type from the case files.

THE UNWELCOMED GUEST

Francine contacted John one day to ask if he could help her get rid of an unwelcome guest. She began, "A few days ago a friend of my 15-year-old daughter, Sofie, who was spending the night, had witnessed a black shape moving into our back bedroom. Earlier that same day, Sofie had also witnessed a black shadow moving by the same back bedroom, but she had first thought that it was me. Even though I was still asleep in a different room, she had not thought of mentioning it to me until her friend saw the same thing."

Francine continued, "Upon hearing this, I remembered that a few years back there had been some strange smells of pipe tobacco and blueberries in the house. Both my husband, Louis, and I had written them off to memories of his deceased grandparents whose house we were now living in. The grandparents had passed around the same time as when we had first noticed the smells." Oftentimes in hauntings, the demonic use familiar smells such as these to mask its presence. This way they can gain the people from the house's trust. With doing this, the demonic can enter the house and the lives of the people living there. Francine then added, "There had been no other instances of paranormal activity until recently."

John made plans to travel to Francine's house, and he was planning on taking the Elwards with him. He felt that Larry may be needed to perform a prayer ritual in this house. He also felt that Debbie's abilities would come in handy in determining what the spirit wanted.

After a tour of the house, Debbie picked up a lot of energy in the back bedroom. She said, "I believe that this is the area that the entity comes and goes through. I feel we should say prayers here.

Larry said "Good...we will say a special prayer that will close up this area." He continued and addressing Francine, "Along with the prayers, may I suggest using some blessed salt around the perimeters of this room? Use just a little as it goes a long way."

John agreed and said "Salt is a natural deterrent against entities. Its crystal properties work to eliminate the energy that is needed to manifest."

As Larry prayed, they all smelled pipe tobacco all though no one was smoking. There was no other outward manifestation during the prayers. It was felt by everyone that this haunting was caught just before it became bad. He finished up by blessing the rest of the house and the outside perimeter of the house. After the ritual, the house felt much better, especially the back bedroom. A week after their visit, Francine called to report that there have been no more black shadows, and that they all felt great, and all were again comfortable in their home.

AUTHOR'S UPDATE:

It has been two years since John's and the Elwards visit to Francine and her family and Francine reports that things are quiet and there have been no more incidences of paranormal activity.

A TALE OF TWO SISTERS

One day in October, John got a call from two sisters who complained of problems in their house. They were sharing a house with their three children. It was an older house in a nice part of town. They had lived there almost three years before they noticed anything strange going on. John planned to travel to their home, and he would be bringing along the Elwards.

The three quickly arrived at the sister's house. They were warmly greeted by the sisters, Amie and Carrie. Carrie, the older sister, began to tell the three about what was going on. "At first things started out slowly with some noises like tapping and knocking which we could always find a reason for it...like old water pipes or the house settling or even critters in the attic and walls." Amie said, "Living in a haunted house was the last thing that we thought was happening to us."

But like most hauntings, the noises escalated and soon were followed by strange smells. It wasn't long before the spirits in the house began to manifest, scaring the sisters and the children.

On the second floor, they would smell a strong odor of perfume around one sister's room. Their three children would be afraid to go to bed at night. Jean, who was seven, would have her hair pulled and her covers yanked while in bed. Her sister, Lilly, who was ten, would complain about the perfume smell in her room. Their brother, Grant, who was twelve, and who slept alone in another room, would experience his closet door opening and closing during the night. The phenomenon was not only centered on the second floor, but the sisters soon began to see spirits on the lower level as well.

While sitting on the couch one night, the oldest sister saw a man's face appear on the landing on the stairs leading to the second floor. Fearing for the children's safety, who were asleep upstairs, she ran up the stairs. As she entered the space where she had seen the face, she noticed that the area felt like a freezer there, even though it was an extremely hot night. She found the children safely asleep.

Amie said: "Another time, I was sitting at the computer in the living room, and I heard a child's voice coming from the enclosed front porch. Thinking that it was one of the children that got up from their bed and was playing on the porch, I quietly got up and walked to the porch."

Amie shuddered and continued, "I did find a child there, but it was not one of mine! This child was a young girl dressed in the turn of the last century clothes. She was playing with a hoop and seemed to be singing a song. She noticed me and slowly disappeared! I was so frightened that I ran upstairs to my own children's room, and that's where I stayed until Carrie, who was working late, came home." Amie said, "After this encounter we felt that we needed help in riding our home of the unwelcome guests. So, we reached out to you all for help."

After listening to the sisters John wanted to do a walk through or a "psychic sweep" of the house. This psychic sweep is when a psychic, like Debbie for instance, goes through the area and picks up any energy in the location that might help identify with the haunting. The three children were staying at their grandparents so they could investigate without worrying about impressionable young ears hearing too much. She picked up that there were many places throughout the house that had a high level of energy. John took many pictures of those various places and was rewarded with many ghost orbs. On the landing of the stairs, he took a picture of a lamp and mirror and got two faces starring back at him.

In one of the children's rooms, a photograph by John showed a large white fog that seemed to stretch over the bed. This was also the room where the perfume is smelled a lot.

Larry put on his vestments and got right to work praying a house exorcism and blessing commanding the entities to leave in the name of Jesus Christ. During the prayers, the house remained relatively quiet there was a few taps here and there, and on the second-floor perfume was smelled. This happens occasionally as the entities prepare to depart.

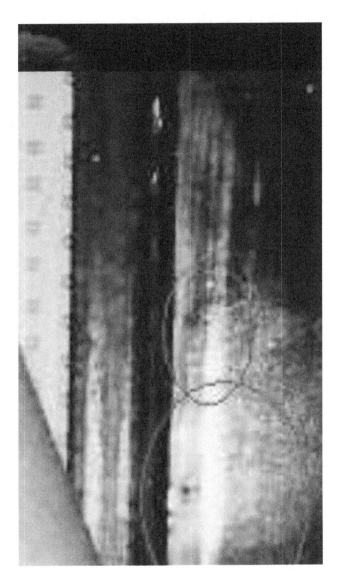

(Above) Faces captured in the mirror

Soon, everything quieted down, and the heaviness seemed to lift as the prayers ended. There was also no discernible smell of perfume. The three packed up and left and Carrie and Amie, who promised to keep in touch.

AUTHOR'S UPDATE:

About a month after their visit, Carrie called up John and told him that the first night, they saw a lot of orbs floating down the stairs and out onto the front porch were they simply disappeared. They did not smell the perfume or see any specters after that. Since John, Larry and Debbie's visit all has remained quiet and there have been no more reported apparitions or noises.

THE MOVED CEMETERY

Sometimes the actions of well-meaning people over a hundred years ago at first may not seem like they would affect lives now a days unless it was an invention or something along that line. But the movement of a small cemetery would not be thought of as effecting this generation, but it did.

Famed showman, P.T. Barnum, was born in Bethel Connecticut in 1810 and died in Bridgeport in 1891. Bridgeport became the home of one of his museums and the winter headquarters of his traveling circus. He built four lavish mansions there, entertaining the likes of Mark Twain, Horace Greeley and other notables of the era. He was also active in local politics, serving four terms as a state representative from the Fairfield area in 1865 and later one term as mayor of Bridgeport in 1875.

Many outlandish tales about the famous showman followed Barnum throughout his lifetime (probably originating from the great showman himself), one of them concerning the moving of a cemetery during his tenure in office. Was the story true or just another one of his many "humbugs" (silly things)? Let us look at one such legend.

Bridgeport was fast becoming a center of industry, and a location near a beautiful seashore would be a wonderful place to build homes for the families of workers employed by the new factories. There was only one problem. A small inconspicuous cemetery was in the way of the grand design. And just by coincidence the mayor (P.T.) owned the area of land adjacent to it. The small cemetery was small and all but forgotten and the new location that was purchased was so beautiful nobody really made much of an objection. Politics won the day and the remains of the deceased who were interred there were exhumed and reburied in the newly purchased plot of land nearby. Or at least most of them were...

As the story goes, the actual exhumations and reburials were done in the dead of night by a man who also worked as a local butcher. He was assisted by some hired hands, who to say the least, were neither conscientious laborers nor respectful of the deceased. Horse carts caring stacks and stacks of coffins traveled thru the city streets. Coffins would fall from the carts, and corpses spill into the streets. Bones scattered everywhere, most of them unidentifiable, only later to be buried in a mass grave. Only the fortunate few were buried with their original headstones. All in all, it was not all that many corpses that got mixed up or left behind and the new cemetery was so beautiful...what could possibly go wrong?

Early one morning, even before the sun was up, John's phone rang and on the other end was a hysterical family. The parents and three children were experiencing the beginnings of a haunting. John planned to meet with them later in the day.

John, accompanied by Larry and Debbie, drove up to their house and parked across the street from their building. As Debbie got out of the car, she said, "I noticed a very heavy feeling that seems to come from the house and into the street." There was actually so much energy that John, Larry and Debbie felt as if they were walking into a fog bank. The woman of the house eagerly met them and began at once to tell them knew what was going on.

Shellie started to tell them, "I have three children. The oldest is a ten-year-old girl named Beth. The next one is a boy named Jed, who is eight. And the youngest, at six, is named, Sara. All three of my kids have reported things happening to them. Beth has had something sit on her bed, and she has always felt as if someone or something is watching her. Jed will hear his name being called when no one is around, and he has seen shadows darting by his bedroom door. Sara seems to have the most happening to her. She is seeing red eyes, hearing breathing, knockings and banging. She always feels a presence in her room and feels as if someone is outside her bedroom window possibly peeking in at her, which is impossible because our backyard is fenced in with a six-foot-high stockade fencing."

Shellie continued, "We have placed blessed devotional candles around the house, especially in areas where this stuff is happening. But when lit they would explode, lights would burn out, and there would be strange smells that would suddenly and unexplainably appear and disappear."

Her husband, Lee, seemed to have been spared any paranormal attacks, but anything that he set down would be discovered moved or missing, causing him to feel tense and irritated. This happens frequently in many haunted houses when one person sees the paranormal activity and the other person does not; usually the woman of the house sees the activity and the man does not. This is done to sometimes cause confusion, and many times, women are more empathic, which spirits are attracted to. They are also attracted to children whose energies are so high level that the spirits feed off these energies.

John explained, "I'd like to do a walk through in your house. This way, I would like Debbie to see what she can pick up. It's not that we don't believe you, but it helps to have her validate what is going on."

As Debbie made her way through the house, followed by John and Larry, she began to tell them of her findings. Debbie said, "The hallway is extremely heavy. The bedrooms and the top floor in the house are also heavy but not as badly as the hallway." She and John went down to the cellar. As they reached the bottom step she turned to John and said, "There is a young man here. He says his name is Joshua. He is a tall, emaciated looking young man. He seems to be around seventeen years of age, and he told me that this land at one time was a cemetery, and that he had been buried there. He believed the year to be 1852 and he told me that he had died of tuberculosis and was buried right where this house is built. He was extremely worried that his family could not come and visit him as his head stone was missing."

John looked surprised and said, "Let's go back upstairs and sit down with Shellie and Lee and tell them what we found in the areas."

John began to tell them about the entity in the cellar. Suddenly Shellie said, "I just remembered a story that I heard of there being a cemetery on this property an exceptionally long time ago and that it was moved. The kids in the neighborhood liked to scare each other with stories about some of the stones in each other's yards being gravestones."

John looked at Shellie and asked, "Is there any physical evidence of this alleged cemetery."

Shellie said, "There are a few strange stone type things in our back yard that we always felt were something to do with horses. Follow me I will show you."

John and the Elwards followed Shellie and her family out to the back yard and Shellie pointed to an oblong stone. John leaned down to examine it and stood up. Turning to the family, he said, "I can see how you would think that this had something to do with a horse and carriage, but sorry to say that this is in fact the foot stone of a cemetery gravestone! So, the stories of this land being a former cemetery seem to check out as being true."

As Larry was putting on his vestments, Shellie asked him a question. "Father," she began. "Aren't these souls that have passed, the ones from this alleged cemetery...I've always believed that they're in God's hands. Do they really care if they get moved after they're dead?"

"That's a good question," replied Larry as he was adjusting his priests stole. "To be sure," he continued, "their souls are indeed in God's hands. But all too often, we forget about the resurrection of the body, which is a cardinal tenet of belief in the religions of Judaism, Islam and Christianity. We were fashioned by God with both a physical body and a soul. But at death, they are separated for a time, and we will only be fully complete when both are reunited at the resurrection. These souls, although they're with God and are happy, are very aware of this separation, hence their concern about how their bodies are treated after their death and why they are sometimes unable to 'rest in peace,' so to speak, when that 'rest' is in some manner disturbed."

John felt that Larry should do a house blessing as well as a blessing for the backyard. He also wanted Larry to incorporate the Prayer of the Dead for all the souls that seemed to be confused and looking for some recognition. He told John and Debbie that he would recite the prayer formula for the dedication of a cemetery thus making the area "Consecrated Ground." He then got out his prayer book and we went about blessing the house and backyard.

Meanwhile, Debbie began the task sending Joshua to the light. She saw "he light" behind him and instructed him to turn around. "Joshua, turn around. I think some people are waiting for you." In this light she saw a man and a woman, presumably his father and mother, standing silently. Joshua turned and walked towards them, and all three disappeared into the light. Debbie is always incredibly careful as to not investigate the light per order of her mentor Ed Warren, as there are some "doorways" too dangerous for psychics.

After Larry had finished up with the prayers, everyone noticed that the house began to feel so much better, and everyone seemed to be more and more relaxed. John told the family that there might be a few noises left, but they will dissipate soon. He said, "Remember these spirits are confused or angry about being displaced as they were. So, it will take them a few days to adjust to what has happened. Just let the prayers soak in."

A few days later, Shellie called John to report that the first night they heard a few knockings but nothing else. The next few nights, she said were quiet and everyone felt more relaxed. She was so thankful to all for their help. Later, John told Larry that it was a nice touch to consecrate the land as a "gravesite." Larry said: "Well, you know I don't like to leave any stone unturned...especially if it's a gravestone!"

AUTHOR'S UPDATE:

A few months later, Shellie phoned John to tell him that all continues to be quiet in their home. She said the kids are not afraid any more in their home. Shellie went on to say that she did some research on the "moved" cemetery. The local legend was not "humbug" after all. In fact, if P.T. Barnum were alive today, he would probably be sponsoring ghost tours!

(Above) John, Larry and Debbie pay a visit to "The Greatest Showman" – P.T. Barnum

RECOGNITION

Everyone wants recognition, whether it is for a job well done, good grades, an outstanding accomplishment - whatever, everyone wants recognition. Even spirits! But giving too much recognition to spirits can be a risky practice.

Graveyards or cemeteries are one of the most highly active paranormal places that there are. Why? Let us think about a graveyard/cemetery for a moment. The living go there to mourn their deceased loved ones. They share with their unseen audiences cherished memories, what is going on in the family , there are many laments over lost loves, as well as too early passing's, and unfulfilled promises and lives. All these thoughts and words go out into the universe as recognition to the deceased. This recognition brings their loved ones to the forefront and sometimes, once this door is opened, something else might wiggle its way into this plane of existence, something that might masquerade as a departed loved one and go unnoticed until it is way too late.

MANITOBA MAYHEM

A woman named Marjorie, from Manitoba Canada, contacted John about some disturbing happenings in her home. She told John, "I went to see a famous psychic about contacting my deceased mother. I was going through a real rough patch, and I felt this psychic could help me contact her...perhaps she could get a much-needed message from my mom. But the psychic told me that I had the power to contact my mother on my own. She told me to put a tape recorder on during the night in order to contact my mom. I did what she told me, and I went to sleep dreaming of contacting my mother. Well, I had made contact all right, but it was not my mother's voice that I heard the next morning when I played back the tape. The voice was a male voice with a British accent that sent chills right through me. The voice said repeatedly 'It smells lovely up close.' I was frightened and a little curious, so I set up the recorder the next night and again I got a voice but not that of my mother. At first the recorder had sounds of giggling laughter, and then there was this raspy voice that said 'Damn pixies' over and over. Also, on the tape there was the English man's voice that said what sounded like 'catharsis'. "Catharsis?" John asked Marjorie, "What happened next?"

Marjorie continued, "I now know it was wrong, but I was still curious and wanted so much to hear my mother's voice, so I felt that if I could get these entities voices on a recording then eventually, I could get my mom's voice. So, I set up the recorder again the very next night. This time it sounded like our poor dog was being tortured! We could hear the agonizing howls upon playing it back in the morning. Whatever it was it did not wake us up that night. The dog sleeps in my room and if he were being hurt in the way that it sounded on the tape, I surely would have woken up. This time I was very frightened and stopped taping." John said, "But unfortunately the damage was done, the door was opened. And now it must be closed."

Marjorie and John made plans for the Elwards and him to travel to Marjorie's house so that they could assist him in closing this "open door" to the other side.

Marjorie greeted her guest upon their arrival. As John and his team arrived at the house the sky was getting dark, and the radio was predicting a severe thunderstorm for the area. What a perfect backdrop for their investigation of this reported haunted house and an even more perfect effect to the planned house exorcism. A very anxious and frightened family greeted the three as they were ushered into their living room.

John as customary asked, "Now has anything happened, Marjorie, since we spoke last." "Well," Marjorie began, "the night before last my oldest daughter, Linda began to see a shadow moving down the hall towards my bedroom. She had been up late studying and was just coming upstairs to bed. Earlier that day, my middle son, Jack, saw what he described as an ancient Chinese or Asian man reclining on my bed as he passed by the door on his way to his room to put his schoolbooks away after coming home from school. Both kids were frightened by these sightings, and everyone began sleeping in one room since then. Everyone is very uneasy in this house. There are tapings and knockings, things became misplaced, and no one is sleeping, and everyone is tired and angry. The kids began to fight... something that they rarely ever did, and their schoolwork is beginning to suffer. Even family members who visit and have tried staying here for any length of time begin to feel the effects of the house and must leave. We have had offers to stay at the homes of others, but I am not comfortable leaving my home, even under these circumstances."

Including Marjorie, there were six people gathered there, and each had the same tale to talk about the dark shadows, the knockings, the misplaced items...the youngest daughter, Lilly, was also attacked by the entity the night before. Her navel was pierced by something and in the morning a clear liquid was oozing from it. Marjorie took her to the doctor who ruled it a bug bite. Lilly denied feeling anything but her cousin, Pamela, who was staying with them, witnessed her sitting straight up in bed staring straight ahead. Yet Lilly does not remember dreaming or doing that.

John decided that Larry should do a blessing over everyone in the house not because he felt that any one person was the target yet, he just felt that it would be the best thing to do under the circumstances. Then he asked him to do an exorcism of the whole house and thus seal the "door" that was opened by the recognition of caused by the recordings. Larry began to pray over the family members, "Bless this vessel of God, Holy Father..." At that moment one of the worst lightning bolts that they had ever seen broke over their heads. The lightening was so bright it illuminated every darkened corner in the room, as it had gotten as dark as night as the storm arrived. The thunder that followed the lightening was so loud it shook the very walls of the house. It almost seemed like as every time Larry said the name of "Jesus" during prayer, there was a loud thunderous boom that shook the walls as if the Lord God Almighty was trying to shake the entities from this house.

As he was praying over the family, Debbie noticed the dog looking up at the stairs. She made her way to the stairs to see what had caught the dog's interest. There on the stairs she saw what appeared to her as a gray blob. She stared at it and noticed that it began to look like a person standing there, it was all hunched over. She could not make out the face but noticed that it had long tapered fingers that rested on the banister. As she was watching this entity, suddenly the oldest daughter became very agitated and she started to cry hysterically saying, "I see its hands... I see its hands!"

Debbie sat down about halfway up the stairs and the thing seemed to move up to the top of the stairs by the bathroom. The dog suddenly pushed past her as she sat on the stairs. He seemed to become increasingly agitated. She got up and stood looking down the long hallway. Suddenly the dog charged past her and down the hall towards one of the back bedrooms. She got up and followed.

Debbie could see a shadow materialize between the two rooms, but she could not see where the dog had gone. Suddenly, out of his mistress' room the dog charged straight for her, barking and growling. He came running down the hall and began attacking her. He began leaping onto her scratching, snapping and growling at her as if she were an intruder in his home. When they arrived, the dog had rushed out to meet them with his tail wagging a cheerful greeting, as if they were long lost friends. Now he had turned and was trying to defend his home against something and was taking it out on Debbie. She tried in vain to push him away, but he kept coming back at her, finally she was able to yell for help and be heard above the raging storm. One of the family members came and got the dog and brought him downstairs.

Marjorie was shaken by the dogs' actions, "Are you alright Debbie? He has never acted like that before! I am so sorry!" She assured them that she was fine. All she had were a few scratches where the dogs' nails had scratched her, but the dog had not bitten her.

The thunderstorm continued unabated while all of this was going on, giving the already oppressive house an even more sinister glow about it. It seemed to have reached its peak as Rev. Larry and John made their way to exorcise the house.

Everyone sat quietly while they went through the house with incense, holy water and blessed salt. But the house was not as quiet...there were the sounds of walking in the kitchen, cold spots would erupt simultaneously around them, strange putrid smells would drift through the room, the dog would stare off and watch some unseen entity walking about, growling lowly in his throat, all the hair on his back bristling up as he hunched over... ready to lunge at his unseen foe.

One of the kids looked outside at the storm and reported excitedly that they had witnessed red lightening over their house. But soon everything became quiet. The heavy air in the house, that when they first arrived seemed like they had just walked into a bar where there had been too many smokers, now seemed clear and fresher. The storm stopped abruptly, and the dog quieted down.

Larry finished the house exorcism prayer with, "Through Christ our Lord, Amen." Everyone commented on how much better they felt that their energy seemed to be returning. John cautioned them, "Don't do anymore taping and don't talk about what's happened even amongst yourselves. Because if you do, the spirits will take it as a sign of recognition, and they've gotten enough of that stuff already." Everyone assured John that they would not and the three departed for home.

AUTHOR'S UPDATE:

Marjorie contacted John after a few months. She told him, "After you left everyone admitted that they were nervous and that they all tried not to concentrate too much on what had happened. So, everyone settled down and tried to sleep. I was awakened in the middle of the night with the feeling of a presence in my room. I felt something get on my bed and felt the pressure of hands on me. Whatever it was started scratching at me and my night gown was shredded. I scrambled out of bed and turned on my light only to find myself alone. I did not sleep the rest of the night. My oldest daughter was frightened but reported no paranormal events."

John had told Marjorie that the thing might escalate after they left, but that they would die down and eventually go away.

That is exactly what happened and slowly she and her children learned to relax in the house and to believe and accept that things were gone for good. Since doing that all is quiet, there are no more nocturnal visits from any entities.

THE MIDWEST ENTITY

A young woman, Ginny from the Midwest, contacted John through his web site. She needed some help dealing with some paranormal activity. John called her right away to find out what was going on. Ginny said, "My boyfriend Rick and I and our young daughter, Bethann, have recently moved into a new house. At first there was nothing out of the ordinary, but a few weeks after moving there I was sitting on my patio and Bethann's bike moved all by itself. At first, I thought that it was the wind, but I noticed that there was no wind. So, I took the bike inside and again sat and watched it and again it moved. This happened quite a few times; by the time Rick had come home I was really excited about this and could not wait to show it to him. So just like in the movie "Poltergeist", we both sat and watched the bike move on its own. Soon after, other things began to happen. My touch lamps would go on as if some unseen hand had touched them. I even unplugged them thinking it was a short... but they still lit up. And soon after that I began to hear voices and music while I worked at my computer. Some of the voices sounded like they were coming from the radio and the television even when they were turned off. Intrigued...I contacted a psychic and she told me to tape the voices, that they were not harmful and that they must have a message for me. She also instructed me to ask the spirits to answer questions and then wait and see if they would answer on the tape. I did as instruct, still believing that these spirits would not harm me or my family."

John interrupted Ginny, "Well, what happened with the recordings? What did you get?" Ginny replied, "At first all I got was strange sounds as if someone were moving around and the recorder was picking up on these sounds. This went on for about a month, then I started to hear what sounded like whispers. This was just about the time when things began to progress fast. Soon I was hearing more than I bargained for on the tapes. I could hear a marching band on the tape that I had not heard otherwise. One tape sounded like a party was going on in my house as we all slept in our beds."

Ginny continued, "I finally did what the psychic had asked me to do. I taped and asked questions. In the morning I played back the recording to hear what, if anything, I had gotten. But the voice on the tape was not Casper the Friendly Ghost! It sounded guttural... like a demonic voice. At first, I could not hear what was being said...but soon there were some more voices that joined the first one. Pretty soon I realized that I did not even need the tape recorder to hear the voices. I could hear them clearly in every room of the house. My bedroom closet is the worse and I feel that this is maybe the center of the haunting."

John said, "From what you are telling me it sounds like a door has been opened and must be closed. I'll assemble a team and we'll get to your house in the next few days."

John contacted the Elwards and a few days later they arrived at Ginny's house. Both Rick and Ginny greeted them and ushered them into the living room where they found little Bethann playing with her dolls. Ginny said, "My mother is going to stop by and pick up Bethann as we don't want to talk about this in front of her and scare her."

After Bethann was safely at her grandmother's, John asked, "OK...so what's been going on since we spoke a few days ago?" Both Rick and Ginny looked at each other and Rick nodded and said, "Go ahead...tell them everything." Ginny looked at her guests and said, " Well...these voices told me that they were my friends and some even said they were my deceased relatives. Two of the voices told me that their names were Randy and Sandy and that I had been reincarnated and that they knew me in a previous life. They told me that I had been killed along with my ten children. The entity calling itself Sandy really seemed to despise me for some reason, and I soon began to fear for my safety, as well as my daughter's. I soon began to feel that I was being watched. No matter where I would go in the house I felt ill at ease. It got so that I could not even go into the bathroom without hearing their cruel comments. Finally, the other day the voices told me that I was going to die...they even gave me the date of my death, which was that night. I already could not sleep as I feared every little noise that I heard, and I even began to fear leaving the house. On those rare nights that I could sleep I had to keep the lights on as well as the television to block out the voices."

John said, "You know the things the voices told you about dying...that was to scare you." Ginny continued, "I know that now, but on the date that the voices had told me that I would die, that night I was so terrified that all I could do was to sit in my kitchen afraid to move, not knowing what to expect. Late in that evening I heard the ambulance coming down our street. It raced into the neighbors across the street. I got up and watched from the front windows as the attendants wheeled our neighbor to a waiting ambulance. Out of the stillness of the house I heard a demonic voice that said, 'Next time it will be you!" I did not know who or where to turn to, as my family and friends, other than Rick and my mother of course, were of no help. They did not believe me about either the voices or the threats. All they thought was that I was mentally ill and that I needed to be in a hospital where I could get some much-needed treatment. I felt that I was at the end of my rope and that soon I would be dead, either from fright or that the spirits would kill me. So, I spent hours on the computer looking for someone that would believe me and get me the help that I needed. " She got teary eyed and seemed on the verge of tears as she said, "When I contacted you and you believed me, I was overwhelmed with joy. I could actually see an ending to this nightmare!"

John explained to her, "What we'd like to do is to make a tour of your house, so we can target any areas that might need more specialized prayers done there."

Ginny, Rick and their three guests did a walkthrough of the house. As was expected by John and the Elwards, areas were located where Ginny spent most of her time, and the noted high levels of negative energy. John explained, "In the areas that you, Ginny spend the most time is where Debbie is feeling the most negative energy. This is where the entities spend a lot of time there with you!" John continued, "I want Rev. Larry to focus his prayers at these spots, then I want him to do a prayer of exorcism over you." She looked almost horrified and said, " EXORCISM!?!" John quickly said, "It's just a prayer, but powerful prayer. Technically it is an ancient prayer asking for Gods healing and blessing. Do not get caught up in the Hollywood hype. It is all about healing...not horror! If you want these things gone, this is the way to do it."

She knew John was right and agreed to be prayed over. Before he began the ritual, Rev. Larry asked her, "Keep us posted as to what's going on inside and how you're feeling...OK?" Ginny just sat there quietly; her eyes closed and face calm. As he went through the ancient ritual, she reported that the voices had gone quiet; they seemed to be no more. She also remarked how much lighter she was feeling. Rev. Larry finished praying over Ginny and then methodically went throughout the house praying the prayers as well as utilizing the ancient sacramental of holy water, incense and salt. He made sure to be extra diligent in the 'hot spots' where the negative energy had been detected. Debbie remarked how much better the areas felt so they packed up their things and left promising to keep in touch.

John has kept in touch with Ginny. She reported that over the last couple of months the voices seemed to grow quiet and now she hears only an occasional sound. Occasionally, the entities try and turn her lights off and on, but she ignores them, and they suddenly stop. Since John's initial visit she has found out that a very abusive former (thankfully) minister once had owned her house. This man was so evil that he would throw things at the children and put out poison for any animals that would enter his yard. The locals stayed away from him because of his meanness. He kept to himself and kept all the shades drawn in his house. Small wonder these things happened in her house. John advised her to keep all the shades open and to let in God's light. He also told her evil hates happiness so try and maintain a cheerful and loving home, which she has done.

AUTHOR'S UPDATE:

John recently heard from Ginny all though things quieted down for a while, she reports that occasionally, the voices start to act up again. It is like they are testing her to see if she will give them any recognition. But instead of being afraid she now is much stronger and much more knowledgeable on how to handle these entities. Now she gets out her holy water and starts to pray. And she knows not to record them or to give them any recognition, so she ignores them for the most part, and the episodes do not last that long. She credits John and the Elwards with saving her life, but John knows that because her faith and determination to gain control of her life and get rid of these evil entities, she was the one that made it possible.

THE NON-BELIEVER GETS PROOF

Sometimes we get more than we hope for...and such was the case of a man from Massachusetts who contacted John last year because he was hearing footsteps that would seem to come in through his front door. As hard as he tried, he could not catch his intruder. "You see," said Timothy, "I don't believe in this ghost nonsense. I am sure that it is an actual person...you know a real living breathing, human being that is toying around with me. We recently moved into this house...a new house and a new town." He continued, "This house is a bit removed from the more commercial parts of town, it's not too isolated but on the other hand, our neighbors aren't too close either, and well to be honest, my wife Bethany was a bit scared the first few nights here. I mean...it is so quiet that once everyone is settled down for the night, you can hear a pin drop. Bethany was used to living in a busy, sprawling town, where the neighbors were so close that if you sneezed in your own house, even with all window and doors closed your neighbor said 'gesundheit!' ha ha-ha!"

John chuckled and interrupted Timothy and asked, "So what happened with the footsteps?"

Timothy replied "At first it sounded like the front door would open, then there was the sound of heavy boots walking across the foyer toward the stairs. I jumped out of bed and ran downstairs thinking someone had broken in. But no one was there. I was sure I would be catching someone...that is someone alive. But last night it got a bit unnerving. Therefore, I called you today.

The footsteps started as usual coming in the front door, walking across the foyer and coming up the stairs and down the hall, where they stopped outside my bedroom door. Then I heard footsteps inside my room, but my door did not open. My wife and I just lay in bed there for a minute and then there were these loud knocks. They seemed to be coming out from the walls. All the walls...every one of them! This was unnerving to me, and Bethany and the knockings woke up our kids

28

scaring them. We have two little ones. John, I really do not know what to think any more! I mean... I am not totally set on this being a ghost, but I do not know what to think. Can you help us?"

John said, "Yes Timothy, I along with my team will be there later today. I'll be bringing a priest and a psychic with me to see what we can do to help you."

"A psychic? Aren't psychics a lot of hooey? I mean aren't they just in it for the money?" asked Timothy.

John said, "There are some psychics that are out to scam people, I'll admit it, but the there are many true legitimate psychics like the one I am bringing today, who are ready and willing to help others and who ask for nothing in return."

Timothy agreed to the help and John planned to meet with Timothy and his wife, Bethany later in the day. He had asked Timothy to have their two little ones out of the house while he and the Elwards conducted their investigation. They had been scared with the activity last night and John did not want to add to it.

Once at Timothy and Bethany's home, John and the Elwards sat down with the couple. The home was a lovely two-story house surrounded by a large yard. It appeared to be well cared for and felt homey. After an initial walk through in which Debbie could not detect any negative energy anywhere. The three sat down to interview the couple. Timothy said, "This is so hard for me to accept! I do not believe in ghosts or spirits or even God for that matter. Do not get me wrong...I have always wanted to believe in something, anything really... especially for proof that there was a God. I felt that this was necessary, especially after our children were born. But no matter how much I asked God and tried to believe I never got any real proof that there was a supreme being. I felt it was useless to believe, or to have that hope at least. So, I dropped my wanting proof. My wife Bethany does believe and has stood by me in my non-belief."

Bethany said, "I don't want to say my husband is wrong, but you know, I see how desperately he's wanted proof yet hasn't received any, so I just let it be."

John looked at the couple and nodded to the Elwards and said, "Well Timothy, I'd say that you got your proof. Debbie has made a thorough 'walk through' of your house, and she does not feel any negative energy. So, I would say, the footsteps and the knockings are your proof of the supernatural. They are, to say the least, your wake-up call."

Larry agreed and said, " We feel that these spirit noises, although scary, are benign and what you needed to show you the existence of God, for without God, the supreme being, once you're dead, you'd just be that.... dead. No footsteps, no knockings....no nothing. As you said it would 'be so quiet you could hear a pin drop.' For you now to get rid of them, you must believe in God."

John said, "We know it will take you awhile to process all this, but it's a must to stop this before it goes too far. A nonbeliever is an ideal breeding ground for demonic infestation and believe me you do not want that. You are lucky you recognized this before it became too much to handle. So, I think I will have Rev. Larry say a quick house blessing and we will be on our way. But we will follow up with you to see how you're doing." Rev. Larry walked through the house reciting some psalms from a prayer book while sprinkling the rooms with a little holy water. John concluded the investigation by saying, "Timothy and Bethany, you can call me anytime with questions or if you need anything."

AUTHOR'S UPDATE:

Over the next couple of months Timothy slowly began to believe. He read the Bible and learned to pray. He and his family joined a church and had the children, as well as him and his wife baptized. He called John recently to report that the footsteps and the knocking had stopped.

AN IRISH CONNECTION

Clara had just gotten back from Ireland. Exhausted but happy, she unpacked the treasures she brought back. Each treasure brought back a memory of what she felt was a place where she eventually wanted to retire. The little peat cottage was her favorite. Just opening the top and smelling the aroma of the peat flooded her soul memories of the Emerald Isle. Sighing, she undressed and got into bed...ready to dream of her second home...Ireland.

She awoke the next morning feeling refreshed from her slumber and got ready to start her day by heading down the hall and into the kitchen to make breakfast. On the floor near the spare bedroom, she found the room's doorknob just lying there. Puzzled, she picked it up and went to look for a screwdriver to put the doorknob back on. After that minor repair she continued with her daily routine, as she had a few errands to run before she could relax. Her day passed quietly without anything out of the ordinary happening and forgot about the fallen doorknob.

The next morning Clara made her way to the kitchen and found the door to the bathroom locked. There was a lock on the inside but there is no way to lock it without being inside the room and locking the door once it is closed. She knew that there was no way to accidentally hit the lock. She had to literally take the door jamb apart to unlock the bathroom door. Puzzled, she began to wonder what was going on in her house.

Later that evening as she was sitting on her couch watching TV, her cats were curled up next to her. One of the cats got up slowly and jumped down to the floor, sitting in front of Clara and stared at the foot of the stairs. The other cat soon joined the first one, both now staring at the foot of the stairs, where she distinctly heard a footfall on the last step. She looked...no one was there. The cats seemed to be following something that she could not see. Soon the cats jumped back up next to her and fell back to sleep. Nothing happened the rest of the night.

Clara decided to go shopping for some much-needed shorts for working in her garden. The weather was getting warmer, and her jeans were becoming too warm. She first tried to go out her back door but found that the doorknob to that door was off, as was the doorknob to the front door was off as well. She again replaced these doorknobs before she could leave. After finishing she headed to her favorite consignment store that just happened to be having a sale. She found three pairs in her style and happily checked out. She finished her errands and headed home. There she threw the three pairs of shorts into the washer and dryer. Later she went down to begin to fold the laundry, she placed a pair of the shorts, a tan pair, on top of the dryer to wear later. She then turned back to finishing folding the rest, she turned back to get the shorts and they were gone. She looked all over the laundry room but could not find them, she even retraced her steps thinking perhaps she was mistaken about the shorts all along, but she was not. As strange as it seemed she even checked the receipt from the store, thinking as bizarre as it seemed perhaps, she had only purchased two pair, but clearly the receipt showed three pairs. One pair was gone. She could not understand what was going on in her home. She did not feel comfortable anymore. At night she would feel like she was being watched as she sat in her living room watching the evening news. Her two beloved cats would seem to be watching someone or something that she could not see. They could be asleep next to her on the couch and suddenly they would whip their heads around looking at the bottom of the stairs, their tails would twitch in annoyance of whatever had disturbed their peaceful slumber.

Things were becoming increasingly difficult for Clara to do any kind of daily activities. If she planned to go out the next day, she would not be able to sleep because of the knockings, rapping's and constant banging of doors. Lately the entity had begun to call out her name in the middle of the night. At first the name was called softly almost as if a mother was trying to gently awake a sleeping child, soon they became more and more insistent in their urgency to alert her. Last night was the last straw, as once again Clara heard her name being called by this time it sounded like her beloved grandmother, when she arose from bed at the calling of her name, and finding not her grandmother, who had passed many years passed, she began to sob and that is when she heard maniacal laughter.

That is when she decided to get some help, she did not want this to go any farther so far things were not bad but now the events seemed to have taken on a more personal theme and she did not want it to escalate any further. So, the next morning she made a phone call to John Zaffis.

John had just sat down at his computer to go over the morning emails. He likes to get an early start on the emails because he never knows when there might be an email that is of an urgent nature. As he was turning on his computer his land line rang, taking a sip of coffee he picked up the ringing phone. Clara was surprised to hear a friendly voice on the other end, she did not know what to expect when she called but was relieved to hear John's warm hello.

Quickly she told him of what was going on in her home. He told her that he would come out later that day with his team to see what was up with the activity in her home and how he and his team could help her.

Hanging up from Clara, he immediately contacted the Elwards to get them on board with the investigation. They as always were eager to get going and to help Clara resolve what was going on in her home.

It did not take long to travel to Clara's house which was located on a non-descript street. By the neighboring houses one could gather that this section of town was where the employees of the neighboring factory had lived, the factory had unfortunately gone out of business many decades previous, but the houses remained as to a testimony to the families that had lived there. Her house was a lovely two-story gabled home that boasted a large porch that wrapped around to the back and led to a Victorian garden, and she told her guests that her garden was both aesthetic and useful. Many of her plants showed signs of a prosperous vegetable harvest.

After a quick tour of the garden, which seemed to be her pride and joy, all settled comfortably in her cozy living room. John began, "Clara I did not share with Larry and Debbie what you had said to me on the phone, I would like to have you start at the beginning and tell them what, when and where you first noticed the activity."

She looked at her three visitors and began, "The first incident was when I returned from Ireland, which was a month ago. I had gotten up early the first morning I had gotten back as I wanted to finish unpacking. I got up and went into the kitchen and found the doorknob to the spare bedroom lying on the floor. I really did not think too much about it as I found a screwdriver and fastened it back on. Nothing out of the ordinary happened that day I went about my daily chores and again went to bed."

She took a sip of her iced tea and began again, "the next morning I got up around the same time as the day before and I found the bathroom door locked. You cannot lock the door unless the door is shut and you physically turn the lock from inside, there is absolutely no way of locking it from the outside. I had to take the door completely off the hinges and out of the door jam in order to open it. Still, I never thought it was anything of a paranormal nature, I just well I just thought it was weird that is all. Later that same evening I was sitting on the couch and was watching some TV before I went upstairs to bed. My two cats were laying on the couch on the side of me, Missy my black and white cat jumped down off the couch and starred at the food of the stairs, Honey my other cat followed suit. As I looked towards where the cats were looking, I distinctly heard what sounded like a footfall on the stairs. I held my breath, but I heard nothing else. Both cats then jumped back up on the couch curled up and went back to sleep as if nothing happened. I sat for the longest time waiting to hear something else. But there was nothing, so I sort of laughed to myself and said 'those crazy cats have me thinking I am hearing footsteps. I shook my head and went to bed not really giving it another thought."

She looked at her three guests and continued. "Now I am a staunch New Englander I got up the next day not really thinking about what had gone on the night before, but still I kept it in the back of my mind. Since it is getting warmer, I made a trip to my favorite thrift store for some shorts for working in my garden. I found three pairs of shorts and came home and threw all three pairs in the washer. When they were finished washing, I took out all three pairs and placed them in the dryer. I was eager to get them done and get out to my garden. When the dryer finished, I took out one pair of shorts to wear and proceeded to fold the other two pairs. I reached for the first pair that I had taken out as I had placed them on a table to go upstairs to change and I could not find them. I looked all over the table, the floor, behind the dryer, in the dryer every place in the laundry room, but I could not find them, they had vanished. I even retraced my steps thinking I had misjudged placing the three shorts the machine, but I could not find the shorts. I even looked at my receipt to see if I had purchased three pairs of shorts and I had. I began to feel extremely uncomfortable in my own home; it did not feel safe to me. At that time, I was thinking that perhaps someone had somehow managed to come into my house and was perhaps playing games on me. I feel as if someone or something is watching me, even my cats are wary of what is going on. I hope that you all can help me. I do not feel safe anymore!"

John turned and looked at Debbie and Larry and said, "Well the first thing I would like is for Debbie to do a walkthrough of your house. It's not that we don't believe you as to what you claim is going on in your home, but we would like to have Debbie, who is psychic to see what she can pick sometimes these things hide from the homeowners and she is able to psychically pick up on them." Clara readily agreed to let Debbie wander the home.

In the upstairs of the home especially in Clara's room Debbie was able to discern an entity that tried to hide itself, she Debbie was able to identify it. She discerned the entity of a young woman. She seemed to be of a by gone era. She had beautiful red hair that was neatly braided down her back. She wore a long dark colored dress that fell just to her ankles. Her face showed signs of hard work, but her eyes were a lovely color green, even in the afterlife they seemed to glow with a brightness that could not be dulled. She then went downstairs to tell the others what she had seen.

Once in the living room Debbie sat down and began to tell what she had seen, "In your bedroom Clara there is an entity, she is a young woman who seems to be lost. She claims to know you as her sister who was lost to this young woman when the sister passed because of a sickness that hit her Irish village, when this young woman realized that you were not her sister it was too late. She had followed you from Ireland and now she was 'lost' and cannot find her way back to her home. I don't think that this spirit realizes that she has passed and that so much time has gone by since she was alive."

John nodded and said, "This seems to happen quite a bit when spirits 'see' a living person that reminds them of someone in their life, they latch on to that living person and when they realize it is not their friend, they become lost and confused. We are not sure why they cannot get back to where they were, but they cannot and must be helped. What I would like with your permission Clara is for Larry to say the prayer of the dead, and Debbie can help to guide this lost soul back to her own plane of existence. Hopefully to convince her to follow the light and seek her family that is waiting for her there. "

Clara eagerly agreed and Larry began the prayer, 'Eternal peace grant onto thee, O Lord and let perpetual light shine upon them may the souls of all the faithfully departed through the mercy of God resin peace. Amen."

As Larry prayed, Debbie psychically homed in on the entity. Quietly, she began communication with the spirit. She told her that there was a beautiful light that was materializing behind the young woman and that many years had gone by since the spirit had been alive. If the woman would follow the light, she would be reunited with her family who were waiting for her on the other side of that light. The spirit was hesitant at first but soon faced the light and began to walk towards it, the closer she got to the light, the fainter she became to Debbie. Soon, the light and the spirit were gone. All was quiet in Clara's home. Debbie could not perceive any spirit energy they were all certain that the spirit had gone. But only time would tell. As the three left Clara promised to update the three.

AUTHOR'S UPDATE:

Clara kept her promised and about a month later she again contacted John to update him on her house. Since the three had left Clara reports that there have been no more visitations from the young woman. No more doorknobs have "fallen" off, and all though the shorts have never shown up again. She is happy that her house is quiet. Her two cats are no longer disturbed by any unseen visitor. Her house is peaceful and quiet.

THE ANGRY MAN'S HOUSE

Father Jacob, who was a priest from a surrounding town, called John to see if he could help a member of his parish with strange phenomenon that was occurring in her daughter's home. Father Jacob at first thought that the daughter, a newly divorced single mother was just feeling the effects of her divorce, being alone with a child in a strange house, so he told his parishioner that he was sending over a friend of his that was an expert in the paranormal.

John called the woman, Monica, to see what he could do for her and her daughter. She was anxious and relived that he would be coming over so he decided to see her later that afternoon and he felt that the Elwards should come with him. He had an idea that Larry's calming presence would make the family relax, and he knew that Debbie would be able to pick up any presence of energy in the house.

John and his group arrived at the house and were greeted by Monica and her husband Neil, their daughter, Emily who lived in the house with her one-year-old son, Brandon. Emily said to the group, "I have lived here a few months and recently I have been hearing footsteps walking up and down the hall, late at night. I am also hearing my name being called no matter which room I am in I get a feeling that I am not alone. My sister, Karen had also lived here before me, but only for a short time and when I asked her if she had heard or felt anything strange, she admitted to a strange feeling of not wanting to be in the cellar alone."

John then said, "Does anyone know the history of this house?"

Monica said, "This house has sort of a sad story behind it. It is one of the oldest houses in this town. It was built in the early 1890s by a couple Mr. and Mrs. Merck. The Merck family has owned it since it was built. The last owners that owned it were the great grandson of the original owner, Carlson Merck, who was a terribly angry man. He would yell at the kids for walking down the street, he seemed to hate the world. When he and his wife, Lydia passed the house went to his older son, Lonny who was unable to keep it due to the large amount taxes owed on it. Eventually the town foreclosed on it. We bought it in a tax sale from the bank. Lonny was so angry and said that he hoped no one would be happy in there, and that one day he would have the house back."

John told them, "Because of the anger of both men, Carlson and Lonny Merck, I feel it is enough to keep the negative energy in this house. Negative energy is not demonic. It is just an energy that is left behind by someone always being negative. It remained even after your family bought it. The negative energy attracted the energy that your family has. This whole house has been 'haunted' by the negative energy. I want Debbie to do a psychic walk through to help pick the areas in this house where the negative energy seems to have accumulated the most. Then I'll have Larry vest up and begin to pray and make an extra effort in the areas that Debbie picks up on."

Debbie started her walk through in the cellar and then went up to the main level and then up to the bedrooms. She returned to the living room to give her report.

"The cellar has an extremely negative feeling to it. It seems that someone spent a lot of time there, being truly angry."

Monica interrupted Debbie. "Sorry to interrupt, but when we bought the house there were still some things left from when Lonny Merck lived here. The bank had a hard time evicting him. We found a lot of his tools, many liquor bottles as well as personal mementos in the cellar. We later found out that Lonny had a serious drinking problem that contributed to him losing his job and his wife and children leaving him. We felt that the alcohol led to him loosing this house."

Debbie also said, "There is a lot of energy on the second floor outside the bedrooms, but it is not as strong as the basement. It just feels like someone keeps walking up and down the hall. The energy is stronger by the large window at the top of the stairs. I feel as though someone spent quite a bit of time there as well as the basement."

Neil said, "That window faces the front of the house. Since there are rumors that Carlson Merck yelled at the neighborhood kids, perhaps that is where he spent his time watching for the kids!"

Emily shuddered and said, "Sorry, but that's sort of creepy! John, can you do anything to replace this negativity in this house?"

John nodded his head and said, "Absolutely! Rev. Larry will say some prayers throughout the house, and both Debbie and I will walk behind him using holy water and blessed salt to counteract the negative energy. Blessed salt works to absorb the negative energy so nothing can manifest in the house."

Rev Larry began his prayers, "Dear God, Holy Father, please send extra angels to this home, and clear away all energy of fear, sadness, or anger. Thank you for infusing this home with your pure loving energy, so that everyone who enters and lives in this house is filled with joy. Amen."

The negative energy began to lift as the three made their way around the house. By the time they made it back to the others in the living room, the atmosphere was noticeably lighter. But Monica was worried that Emily would still be afraid to live in the house. John explained to Emily that she must take her house back. He told her that she was to make this a happy cheerful house and to try and not give any recognition to any noises that she heard. By giving any recognition to the noises, it would give recognition for the negative energy to return.

AUTHOR'S UPDATE:

Monica and Neil contacted John to report that after John and the Elwards initial visit and prayers, things had quieted down in the house. Emily happily reported that she has not heard any more footsteps. She can be alone in the house and to once again feel that the house was her own. This summer, the Monica again contacted John. It had been a few years since his visit to the home. Emily's new husband had been transferred out of the area, and Monica and Neil were going to be renting out the house. She wanted John to come over and to walk through the house to make sure that all negativity was gone so that the new tenants would be sure to have a peaceful home.

John and the Elwards went over that afternoon and the house was fine. They did pray in it to make sure. John has not heard anything from the owner or her tenants, so he imagines everything is fine.

LOST LOVED ONES

Cemeteries can speak to you, through the gravestones, or sometimes through the spirits that inhabit them. These cemeteries hold the earthly remains of people and family and friends who come and give recognition to them by talking of days gone by, wishing that they were with them once again, how much they are missed and to even decorate the graves with things that the deceased loved and cared about. All this gives recognition to the spirit, and with this recognition they can gain the energy needed to manifest themselves. Many times, these people died under tragic circumstances or with something left unfinished. All though cemeteries seem calm and barren to the ordinary eye, to a person who is sensitive, they are a highly active location. So many eras superimposed over each other. A sensitive person might become aware of soldiers from World Wars One and Two, women in old fashioned dresses from the turn of the last century, and men in many different style suits and even children at play.

Sometimes driving to a case John and the Elwards might find themselves diverted to help a spirit in need. Many times, John, Larry and Debbie have driven by a cemetery and had a spirit call to them to come and help them. Sometimes, they can be very persistent as in the following spirit encounter. One such occurrence happened as they drove on the interstate in Southern Connecticut one evening at twilight.

As they drove past, they could see a cemetery just off the exit. The setting sun gave the tombstones an almost ghostly appearance, but that was not what caught Debbie's attention to it. She heard someone call to her as they drove past. At first, she did not tell John or Larry about it, so they kept driving. But again, she heard someone call to her. This time it was louder, but still she ignored the voice. But this spirit was unrelenting, and he continued to call until finally he got into the car with the three. Both John and Larry felt an oppressive heavy feeling that seemed to envelope the car's interior. They got off at the next exit turned back to the cemetery.

During the drive, the spirit communicated to Debbie, telling her that his name was Angus Stanton and that he was worried about his wife. He told her that he was incredibly angry that he had passed and had to leave his wife behind, as she was young at the time. He was worried that she could not manage all alone. They had not had any children to take care of her; he knew that she was all alone. He made sure that she knew that he was angry at God for taking him at such an early age and leaving his young wife alone. But now, his wife too had passed. He was worried that by his being mad at God, he would never be with her again. He desperately wanted God to forgive him so that he could be reunited with his wife once more.

Angus led them to his grave, and they noticed that he was indeed a young man when he passed. He was only 35 years of age and that he had been dead since the early 1940s. They also noticed that his wife, Camille, had passed in the mid-70s. In the spirit realm, time is nothing. What is many years to us feels like seconds to them, so therefore, Angus told them that his wife had just passed, for him. For John, Larry and Debbie, she had been dead over 30 years.

As Larry took out a prayer book and began to pray for Angus' soul, Debbie tried to assure him that God had indeed forgiven him. Soon she saw this very dazzling pinpoint of light that grew larger and brighter as Larry continued to pray.

Soon the cemetery seemed to grow silent and still. No sound could be heard, not even the sound of the traffic going by on the interstate. Time seemed to stand still. For a moment, all Debbie could see was the bright light, which still seemed to grow larger and brighter. Slowly, she began to see a shape of a woman as she stepped out of the light. She told Debbie that her name was Camille Stanton and that she was here to show her husband, Angus the way to the light. At that moment John, Larry and Debbie knew that God had indeed forgiven Angus for his anger. After all is not God our father who loves each one of us and isn't he ready to forgive us for anything if we are terribly sorry?

The last time Debbie saw Angus and Camille, the two of them were walking hand in hand into the light, just as the light slowly disappeared. The heavy oppressive air began to lift and soon everything returned to normal. Once again, the sound of the highway and the crickets could be heard.

John, Larry and Debbie smiled and then they resumed their journey, satisfied with helping a deceased loved ones reconnect.

AUTHOR'S UPDATE:

Much like a moth being attracted to the light of a candle or lightbulb, ghosts and other spirits are frequently attracted to the 'auric' light that emanates from psychics like Debbie. They are often attracted and sometimes want to make contact.

THE LONELY FARMER

In a small town in New York State, Kevin and Linda moved into their dream home. This house had been moved from a nearby town to its present location when the state wanted to flood the area for a reservoir for New York City. This occurred around the turn of the century.

The couple had made many renovations, adding a second story, a front porch, and a kitchen wing. Shortly after all the work was completed, strange things began to happen. Kitchen cabinets would open and close, things would be moved and both Kevin and Linda saw a man standing by their shed, which had also been moved with the house. They both describe the man as looking like a farmer. He was tall with a full beard and was dressed in overalls and was wearing a straw hat, similar what an Amish farmer might wear. He did not move or even acknowledge that he saw Linda and Kevin. Although Linda was not frightened by this man, she felt that he was looking for something or someone. She began her search for someone to help this man find the peace that he needed to move on. She contacted John who felt that he and the Elwards might bring closure to this spirit. He felt that maybe Debbie might be able to communicate with the spirit to see what they could do. He set up a date to meet with her at her home.

The night before John spoke with Linda on the phone, Debbie had a "visitor" at her home. She asked the spirit, "Who are you and what do you want?"

The spirit replied, "My name is James Jamison." He then went on to say that he believed it to be 1900 and that he was looking for someone. He then showed her that there had been an accidental death associated with the shed. The death was caused by a blow to the head and strangulation.

Slowly the vision faded, and all returned to normal in her room, yet she was puzzled by the visitor. Nevertheless, she fell right to sleep. Many times when Debbie receives an apparition, she is so worn out afterwards as she has used a lot of energy. The next day, John called to say he had a case to do later that day, and he wanted the Elwards to go with him. Debbie told him about the vision, and he felt that it had to do with the upcoming case.

It was a short drive to Linda and Kevin's house. As they drove by a large reservoir, John told the Elwards what Linda had told him about having to move their house to make room for the same reservoir.

The house that the three pulled up to was a two-story farmhouse. There was a wide front porch that overlooked the reservoir. There, in the backyard, was a modest size shed that Kevin explained was the same one where he and Linda had seen the man standing.

Linda and Kevin met them as they pulled into their driveway, they seemed eager to get started. Linda said, "After talking with John on the phone, I found out some more information about the man and the house." She continued, "I learned that this man, James Jamison, was a widower and he had two children. And that his two children had died accidentally in the shed. One had been hit in the head and the other had strangled, both on the same day. The day after the funeral of the two children, James, who was extremely distraught by their death, committed suicide. The year was 1900. I also found out that they had moved the church and a lot of the houses, but they did not move the cemetery. It was still submerged in the reservoir. I believe that this is where the children are buried."

John said, "This makes a lot of sense. This James Jamison was so distraught about the deaths of his son, he killed himself. But it's also possible, that in his belief of suicide being a sin, he possibly did not move on, and he is still looking for his children." He then said, "I am going to have Reverend Larry say some prayers for the repose of his soul, plus a blessing of the house, property and all the buildings."

Reverend Larry began the prayers in the dining room and throughout the two floors. Where Linda and Kevin had last seen James, he said a prayer for the dead which is commonly said at funerals, "Rest eternal grant him, O LORD. Rest eternal grant unto them, O LORD, and let light perpetual shine upon them. Amen." As Larry was finishing the last prayer, Debbie "saw" two young boys running towards a now smiling James. She told everyone what she had just seen. John agreed that the prayers had been effective, and that Linda and Kevin should have no more paranormal activity. The three left promising to keep in touch.

AUTHOR'S UPDATE:

   John has kept in touch with Kevin and Linda since their visit and has learned that all is still quiet at their home. There is no more activity and no more sightings of James Stenson, the prayers had worked.

SASSY

Psychic ability almost always runs in families. Debbie's family is no exception. Children especially seem to have more of an ability to see, hear and feel spirits than adults. It is felt that children under five who witness spirits are able to do so because they are not held back from doing so because, simply, they have not been told that it is impossible to see spirits. Children in these age ranges still believe in fairy tales, Santa Clause, the Easter Bunny and the Tooth Fairy. Their belief has not been jaded by non-belief. Their aura is pure and shinning bright, and the spirits are attracted to them.

Debbie's granddaughter, Reagan, seemed to inherit the gift. From an early age, she would have conversations with spirits and even Devine Beings. Her mother, Debbie's daughter, Stacey, who has the gift herself, would be driving past a cemetery, and Reagan would remark in her three-year-old wisdom, "They look so lonely, Momma!"

But Stacey would quickly tell her, "Honey they have to stay here. They can't come with us." But one time the little girl seemed not to have listened to her mother's warning.

Stacey was getting dinner when she heard her three-year-old chatting away in the other room. Stacey went to find out what was going on.

The child's room was chilly, and Stacey immediately recognized the psychic cold that was associated with a spirit being around. She asked Reagan who she was talking to, and the young child answered. "Sassy." She asked Reagan to draw her a picture of Sassy, and she drew a picture of a stick figure with red lines going through her body.

Not liking that, and not wanting to alarm her daughter, Stacey asked the child to send Sassy away. Even though Stacey has the gift, she herself could not see Sassy. She wanted the spirit to go away because she also knew that many times spirits can masquerade as something else than what they actually are.

The air in the child's room immediately returned to normal, and Stacey went back to preparing dinner. Soon her phone rang. It was her mother, Debbie, on the phone.

Debbie asked. "Did Reagan have a visitor?" and Stacey said that she did, but that Reagan had sent it away.

Debbie asked, "And where did Reagan send it?"

Stacey answered "Well since you are asking, I gather your house. Sorry."

Debbie said "Well I just came out of the shower, and I am greeted by this little blonde hair girl. She said her name is Sassy and she is lost. I communicated with her about who she was looking for and she said 'Johnny my brother.

I discerned Johnny, a spirit of a small boy about 8 years old. He said he was Sassy's brother, her name is Sally, but she was such a bright spirited child that everyone called her Sassy.

One day, his father and Sassy and Johnny had gone to the fields to ride on the thresher while their father cut the hay. The thresher was pulled by two big horses, and the young kids loved to ride along with their father. This time, the field was rough with rocks and crevices deep in the soil. The thresher hit a rock, and before their dad could react, Sassy had tumbled backwards into the blades of the thresher, which cut up her young body. She died instantly.

I saw Johnny and Sassy together after that. She had finally found her brother, and I am sure they were reunited with their parents who had passed along with the brother a long time ago.

"Tell Reagan she did good, but no more inviting way ward spirits home," Debbie said and then hung up laughing. "I guess the apple does not fall far from the tree!" she thought to herself.

AUTHOR'S UPDATE:

Even though the decades had come and gone since Sassy's death, her parents had passed, her beloved brother had grown up, had a family of his own, and he too had passed. In Sassy's spirit world, no time had passed from when the accident happened to when Sassy saw Reagan's welcoming glow. No one knows why some spirits become lost or "stuck" on the way. Either she was too scared, or she could not comprehend what happened for her to be able to see the light. And so her spirit wandered, looking for a way to reconnect with her best friend, her brother.

There is a whole new generation of Debbie's family that has begun to exhibit their psychic abilities. Some of the abilities are slow to materialize, but they eventually do, and many abilities become stronger as they get older. They are all aware of embracing or shunning their abilities and have taken the necessary steps to either use them or not. It will be interesting to see how far these abilities will go in the family with each new member.

THE DARK SIDE

Photo by Dan LeRoy Productions, LLC | danleroyproductions.com

CURSES

Dealing with people who have been cursed is nothing new to John, Larry and Debbie. In their line of work, they have seen just about everything that encompasses someone or something having been cursed.

A curse, also called a "jinx" or "evil eye," is defined as a prayer, wish or spell that misfortune will befall or attach itself to a person place or thing. Curses can be often attached to someone simply by just saying the words. Sometimes no ritual or spell is needed, just the psychic energy expended and the mere mention of what you hope for someone is enough to turn someone's life into utter chaos.

At other times, however, full blown rituals involving the four elements of air, fire, earth and water, the phases of the moon, etc., are used depending on the expertise of the practitioner and the desired outcome. It can also involve the invocation of a god or goddess and or elemental spirits. The following stories are cases of curses that they have dealt with over the years.

CURSE OF THE ANCIENT ONES

Gloria grew up in a family with a long line of professors and archeologists. Her father was one and so were her grandfather and great grandfather. In fact, her parents had met while on an archeological dig while in college. Her great grandfather had been on many famous digs and had brought back many fine artifacts from these digs. At the time of her great grandfather, it was permissible for the archeologists to take small nonessential items as a keepsake of the dig.

Growing up, she loved to touch and listen to the exciting stories behind these artifacts that her grandfather would talk about. Sometimes she would let her imagination take over as she listened to the tales, and she would wonder what it must have been like to live in the era that these artifacts were from. Many times, these imaginative thoughts seemed to take over her thought and she'd begin to see scenes from long ago, it was almost as though she were remembering her own past.

One set of artifacts that her great grandfather had acquired was from a dig in Samaria. Samaria is a historical and biblical name used for the central region of the ancient Middle East near Israel, bordered by Galilee to the north and Judaea to the south. As a young child, these ancient lands and cultures had captured her interest, and when her great grandfather passed, he left her a set of artifacts. She had always loved these artifacts. They were almost magical to her and seemed to be able to transport her to a different time and place with the stories behind them. When she left her parent's home, she took these artifacts with her and kept them in a prominent place in her own home to admire them and remember her great grandfather.

As Gloria got older, into her late thirties and early forties, she noticed that she began to have a hard time concentrating and putting words together to make sentences. She went to many doctors and went through numerous procedures and tests, but they could find no medical reasons for her problems. Around this same time, she became very active in a church, something that she had previously not done before.

This church was a small nondescript, non-denominational congregation in her hometown. She loved the camaraderie of the people when they would get together for the adult bible studies, and she soon was having a group of them over to her home. Many times, the pastor, a middle-aged man, would attend these get-togethers.

Many of her guests were interested in the story behind the artifacts that seemed to be at the center of her home. Gloria loved to tell the stories of the different digs that her ancestors had been involved in and how each artifact was once used. One of them, however, drew the pastor's attention. It was a small idol, about three inches high, which depicted a deity whose name seems to have been lost to history. The pastor, who was an amateur history buff himself of those ancient biblical regions, especially that of the area surrounding Samaria, immediately recognized it as being an artifact from the tomb of Haheshe, one of the high priests of the second century BCE. Not too much is known about Haheshe other than he had died under mysterious circumstances. The pastor also heard of a legend that there was supposedly a curse associated with the disturbance of anything in the tomb.

Although the pastor could not decipher the writings on a scroll he found online, he felt that it might have something to do with the alleged curse. He suggested that she had better get rid of these "unholy" artifacts (as he called them) as soon as possible before any harm was done, and the small group left quickly afterwards.

She chuckled to herself. All this talk of cursed objects was superstitious, if not downright silly. After all, her family had been digging for years and nothing had happened to any of them. Gloria did not know it at that time, but she would never see her group of church friends again. And this was the beginning of Gloria's nightmare that would take some time for it to end.

(Above) Gloria's artifacts

That night she had a horrible nightmare. Strange images of far way places swirled around her, and many hands reached out to grab her, as she tried to elude them. She felt herself being dragged along the ground. The next thing she knew she was being sealed into a tomb, as a huge stone was rolled in front of what looked like a doorway snuffing out the light, making her feel like she would slowly suffocate to death. Gasping for breath, she managed to wake up. She was shocked to find that she had many scratches on her arms, legs and torso. There was a fine layer of what looked like sand on the floor. There was some sand on her feet and legs, as well as under her bruised fingernails. It was as if she had clawed her way out of the sand. She thought to herself, "What is happening to me?" But she laughed it off as maybe she had a very vivid imagination. She remembered her childhood and the images she used to conjure up when she played with these artifacts at her great grandfather's house. The next morning all indication of what had happened...the bruises, the scratches and the sand had disappeared, firming her impression that yes, she had just dreamed it all, even the part about the bruises and the sand.

Over the next few years things got worse and slowly Gloria came to the realization that it was something more than her imagination. Her inability to concentrate or to put words together escalated into her being dismissed from her job of teaching. The nightmares became more intense and more frequent. Because of them she could not sleep, as she was too afraid to sleep. Sometimes her hands and legs did not seem to be part of her own body. If she were cutting vegetables in the kitchen her hand would seem take on a mind of its own and try to cut her other hand. Sometimes when she tried to walk in a straight line her legs would act independently of one another and make her stagger and walk in circles. Soon she became too debilitated to leave her home. All her friends turned their backs on her. Her church shunned her. She was left alone to figure out what was afflicting her. She tried in vain to get any help for what was soon becoming a living nightmare. She surfed the Internet in hopes of finding someone that could help her. Still, she was not too convinced that all her problems were due to a curse...but still she began to wonder.

While researching late one night, she came across John's website. With interest, she read about how he had helped many people who were suffering from the throes of paranormal problems. She contacted him the next morning and decided to fly John and the Elwards to her home in San Francisco as soon as she could arrange for them.

Gloria lived in a modest two-story town house in San Francisco's south side. There was no indication from the outside that anything paranormal was going on inside, but John, Larry and Debbie knew that looks can be deceiving.

Once inside, they all sat down, and John began. "Gloria, can you begin by telling us what has been happening to you and when this all began."

She hesitated for a second and slowly began, "It seemed to start around the time that I joined a small church and started having get together with a group of young adults. They liked to come over to my house, and I would show them my artifacts that my great grandfather left to me." She pointed to a shelf over her sofa that held five small statues. She went onto explain "My great grandfather was an archeologist working on a dig in the area of what was once referred to as Samaria. During the time he was there he could bring home small items. When I was a small child, he would tell me stories that accompanied and centered around these particular artifacts. "

Debbie, meanwhile, had gotten up and made her way to the artifacts. She had noticed that there was a large amount of negative energy emanating from them, especially one small idol that was in the center. She picked up and held each artifact for a moment with her eyes closed, discerning any energy that might be associated with each one. "The negative energy seems to circumvent the other four artifacts making them give off a negative aura" she said.

As she pointed this out to the others Gloria looked almost ashamed and said "Yes that is what I have been told by a few people, but I really didn't believe that all my problems could be because of a small artifact! I should have listened. I could have saved myself years of torment!"

John quickly said, "Don't beat yourself up. Let's just get this taken care of." He then suggested Larry to start with the prayers over Gloria and afterwards bless the house.

Larry told Gloria, "I'll start off with a prayer to break curses, both over you and then the artifacts. Then I'll recite a prayer of blessing over you and your home. "

The ritual started with no outward signs from the entity, but a change seemed to come over her. When they first arrived, she seemed a bit tense, but now as the prayers continued, she seemed to be relaxed and calm. Larry finished up praying over her and began going thru the house with holy water and exorcised salt. The entire ritual took only about 30 minutes.

After the prayers were finished Gloria turned to the three and said, "Please take these artifacts and get them out of my house. PLEASE!!!" John agreed and boxed the artifacts along with some blessed salt to dissipate the negative energy.

Gloria thanked them and the three lefts to go back home, taking along the artifacts as requested by her to be safely stored in John's paranormal museum where they remain till this day.

AUTHOR'S UPDATE:

Gloria has kept in touch with John, and she reports things are looking up for her. She has since moved from her home to a new one in a different town. She has joined another church and is slowly putting her life back together. She has had no re-occurring symptoms that she was experiencing before John and the Elwards visit and since removing the artifacts from her home.

THE AFRICAN CURSE

One chilly November, John was contacted by a family from Canada who believed their 20-year-old daughter, Sylvie, was the victim of some sort of curse. After speaking with the family over the phone several times to verify the facts of the case, John, Debbie and Larry traveled to Canada to see if they could help this young woman who was dealing with what appeared to be the effects of what her parents believed to be an African curse. It should be noted that this family had immigrated from Ghana, so they were knowledgeable of such things. This poor girl was afflicted so badly that she was unable to walk and forced to drop out of college. The three arrived in the city of Halifax, Nova Scotia a few days later.

John and the Elwards sat down with Sylvie and her family to find out how this might have started. The mother said, "A classmate who was jealous of our daughter we believe had placed the curse on her in high school." She went on, "This girl pretended to be our daughter's friend, even giving her a few African tribal masks, something that our daughter collected. We believe that this was done just so that she could gain access to our house and get the items that she needed to use for the curse. One of the items that the friend needed was something personal to Sylvie." She paused and seemed to be embarrassed by what she had to say next. "This friend took our daughters used sanitary napkins, her toothbrush and her hairbrush."

According to "Blood Magick" practitioners, menstrual blood, and indeed all blood drawn from a living person, is imbued with life and energy. It is uses can include anointing candles, amulets or added to mojo bags in order to make a spell more powerful. It can also be used as ink to write a spell or used in divination. How it was used in this case was not clear.

(Above) African mask

The father then spoke up. "At first we were unaware of what was going on because the curse was being slowly put on her. We did miss certain items, but a curse was the farthest from our minds. But by the time Sylvie graduated from high school the curse began its full onslaught. Still, we never expected a curse."

The father went on, "As she entered the university, the effects of the curse began to be felt in earnest. Because of our daughters' good academic standings, she was able to attend the university on a full four-year scholarship. The first year that she tried to attend, she was able to register but not be able to attend classes. She began to have severe trouble with her stomach. She would have such bad pains that would render her bedridden, unable to concentrate or to leave the house."

The mother continued: "We sought medical help both for a physical aliment and a mental one, but the tests came out negative for any problems. The doctors performed exploratory surgery in hopes of finding a cause for her pain. But nothing was found that could physically cause her such torment. Shortly after returning home from the hospital, she began to have seizures."

The father added: "Soon, she began to experience other symptoms along with the pain and seizures. She could not keep anything in her stomach and would vomit. She vomited so many times that her esophagus was damaged, and she needed surgery to help repair that. Then she was only able to eat soup in small amounts. A feeding tube was inserted to keep her from starving."

Then the mother said "If all of this were not bad enough, she developed a very sore ulcer on her foot that once again the doctors could find any logical explanation. This ulcer caused her a great deal of pain and soon she became unable to walk. Her father has to carry her everywhere even into the bathroom." Life had become a living hell for her and her parents, who were in upper middle age and nearing retirement. The father had to continue to work to pay the medical bills while her mother, who was a talented seamstress, was fortunately able to work at home since taking care of her daughter was full time job.

Her parents were deeply religious and had prayer groups over to the house to pray for their daughter. During one of these deliverance services the demon came forward and boasted to the family what had happened and what it was going to do with this young woman. The prayer group felt that this was out of their league, so they suggested for the parents to find someone that was experienced in this. One member had seen John on TV and they felt sure that he could offer help for their situation. The next day, the parents contacted John and asked him to come with his team to see what could be done for their daughter.

It was agreed by the team to begin with prayers of exorcism. Larry explained to the family what this would entail and told Sylvie to interrupt the prayers at any time if she felt ill or noticed anything demonic or paranormal occurring. The young woman sat quietly listening to the prayers. Occasionally she would pray quietly "Help me Jesus," but then she became quiet and lowered her head for a while. When she picked her head up, she looked like she was in a lot of pain. She began to grimace, and her face began to distort. She started to drool and then she began to call out in a language that sounded like some sort of African dialect. Many times, she cried out "Nee! Nee!" which means, "No! No!" She began to call for one of the demons that possessed her; "Mbwiri! Mbwiri!" she screamed its name repeatedly. (Mbwiri is an African demon that inflicts pain and causes epileptic seizures.) It was as if the other demons were looking for this one demon. Again, a voice cried out "Shiboka!" which was translated later and means, "I exist for you!" Soon, she began to talk nonstop in this language, and she began to rock back and forth. Mixed in with all of this, she also was calling out for Jesus to help her. Awhile later a different voice said, "Nigikhona" meaning: "I am here!" Still Larry continued to offer prayers on her behalf. Suddenly a gravelly voice said" Uhambekakuhle!" which translates to, "goodbye."

She became quiet, the talking stopped, as did the rocking. The poor girl looked worn out. Larry finished up the ritual with a final blessing of all those present and the three left the family to let the young woman rest. That evening the mother called and reported that the young woman had been able to have some soup and to keep it down, this was the first time in weeks that she had been able to do that.

After returning home, the mother has kept in contact with John to report that the young daughter was getting better each day. She has been able to take a few steps. The family continues to pray and ask the Lord to heal her completely.

AUTHOR'S UPDATE:

John has kept in touch with this family, and they report that their daughter has returned to the university and is getting on with her life, hoping to put this horrible experience behind her. The family also reports that they are sending the African mask to John's museum for safe keeping, so that no one else meets its evil. About a week after their return from Nova Scotia, John received the African mask in the mail. As he normally does, he placed the mask in an outbuilding until he can arrange for prayers to bind the spirit. Upon entering the outbuilding, he was met by a complete disaster, things that were still in boxes had been ripped from them and thrown about, as were other artifacts housed there before putting them into his museum. This was the first time that something like this had ever happened and nothing like this has happened since. So, John is sure that whatever energy or power that was in this mask was immensely powerful and very dark. It is now in John's museum and is protected by numerous prayers and rituals to keep it energy in check.

DRUID CURSE

Margaret, an active middle-aged woman, contacted John one Advent season with a problem. She stated that she was having trouble from spirits that she felt she had picked up on one of her many trips to Ireland. Margret told John, "During Mass recently, a strange sensation came over me. Before I could stop myself, I began talking in an unknown language, which someone later identified as Gaelic, the Irish language. I kept saying over and over 'Dioltas dioltas,' which I later found out that in English it means 'revenge!'" The pastor was shocked and really did not know what to make of it. Thinking it may be an emotional or mental problem, he politely suggested Margaret not to attend any more services at his church until she "felt better."

Fearing that there was possibly something spiritually wrong with her, she made a search over the Internet and came across John and his team. Immediately, she contacted him, and soon John, Larry and Debbie traveled to her home in New Hampshire to interview her and to pray with her.

Margaret said "I've traveled extensively to Ireland, visiting many of the ancient ruins of the Emerald Isle. Many of the sites that I have visited were once Druid worship sites. I found these the most interesting to me. I must admit that at one site, I stumbled upon a small and strangely shaped stone that was on top of a cairn. (A cairn is a manmade pile or stack of stones. These cairns have shown up in prehistoric times all the way up to present modern times. There are many reasons for these cairns, from showing a way for hikers and possibly in this case some sort of ritualistic symbol). The stone felt cool to my touch and seemed to give off a pulsation that I found intriguing. I was so mesmerized by this stone that I slipped it unseen into my coat pocket. I then traveled home and did not really give it too much thought. I did put it on a shelf in my living room and forgot about it, but shortly thereafter things began to happen, leading up to the recent incident at church."

She seemed to have no other problems associated with her visiting these sites, but possibly due to taking the stone, John felt that whatever was going on was in just the beginning of what is known among exorcists and paranormal investigators as the "infestation" stage. The infestation stage is where a spirit starts to make itself and its agenda known. This is what may be termed as "'haunted house syndrome." It can manifest as footsteps, voices, apparitions, furniture or objects moving by themselves or odors with no discernible source. He decided to pray over her and to see if this would help her.

As Larry began to read the exorcism prayers, Margaret began to fidget in her chair and soon was exhibiting the classic signs of the presence of a possible spirit. Suddenly, a voice with an Irish brogue came out of Margaret. At first it was staggered words, but as the spirit took over her, it began to form a picture of what was going on. The spirit said "Is leasta me'!" Loosely translated to English means, "You are mine!"

Debbie looked around the room and said, "I thought I heard a baby crying." The spirit told of many sacrifices to the Druid gods and one sacrifice where a young baby had been killed in honor to a god. Margaret began to cry and told us in her own voice that when she was in her early twenties, she had found herself pregnant and alone and had gotten an abortion. The father of her child was a Lutheran minister with a wife and small children and would not leave his family for Margaret and their unborn child. Later, when she had the means, she had traveled extensively in Ireland to various old churches and pilgrimage sites in the hopes of atoning and/or forgetting her past mistake.

She was sorry and felt that possibly she had made the decision after she had returned from a trip to Ireland to one of the Druid sites. She felt that if she had not gone there that possibly she would have had the child and not have aborted it. She felt that perhaps the energy of the area had somehow affected her in her decision-making process. After this confession and prayers for emotional healing, Margaret believed that the spirit had left her.

AUTHOR'S UPDATE:

Since their visit Margaret reports that there have been no more problems with spirits in her life. She is busy working with unwed mothers to help them find an alternative to abortion. She has also sent the stone back to the site where she picked it up. Life is looking up for Margaret once again.

AMERICAN INDIAN CURSE

Cynthia, a "thirty something" woman, called John in the summer of 2003. She said on their initial phone conversation, ".... that for most of my adult life I have been plagued by what I believe to be evil spirits that would not allow me to have any kind of meaningful relationships. I have been to many doctors, both medical as well as psychiatrist, to alleviate my debilitating condition. There was never any medical or psychological condition found to cause these conditions."

Cynthia was unable to perform day to day activities. On many days she found she could not leave her home to go to work, or to the store, or to even take a simple stroll outdoors. Her condition left her unable to maintain a friendship or any close ties to her family.

With money that she inherited from her parents, she was able to purchase a small home and to be able to live as a semi reclusive soul. Still, she hoped to be freed from this life of solitaire and to become a vibrant individual, free to do what deep in her heart she felt was the life she was meant to live. She went onto tell John, "As far back as I can remember, I've always felt as if I was not alone in my thoughts. I have always felt as if I was being watched and directed by some unseen force. I contacted you, John, hoping that you might help rid me of this feeling and to get on with my life."

On their first face to face meeting John asked, "Cynthia could you please fill us in on a little of your childhood background, just so we can figure out what is going on."

She said, "As a small child, my parents and I spent our summers in a mountain cabin in the Black Mountains of South Dakota. There was a local folklore that this cabin might be on sacred Indian ground, possibly from the local tribe that many years previous had been numerous in population in that area. It was shortly after my parents had passed that I began to experience some of these problems. I feel that somehow something had been disturbed on the property where the cabin was, and that this is when the spirit began to invade my life and make it what it has become today."

John agreed that the team would pray with her and see what they could do in helping her to rid her of this evil presence that they felt was infringing on her life. As Larry began to pray over her, she began to manifest in a strange voice, it seemed to be that of an ancient Indian spirit. This spirit at first began to speak in its native language calling out "Watokico!" which loosely translates into 'avenge' in English. Soon, the spirit talked in broken English as it began to tell a story of what had happened to cause it to want to reach out and cause this woman so much grief in her life.

Cynthia and her parents had indeed lived in a cabin situated on very sacred Indian land. This land was used by the shaman of the tribe as a place of prayer and sacrifice to their Indian gods for the health and prosperity of the tribe. Besides, an Indian burial ground plot of land was the second most sacred place to the Native American.

But Cynthia conflicted with the spirits because she and her parents had lived on this land. The spirit explained that as a young child, Cynthia had defaced the sanctity of this ground by urinating on it. The ancient spirit felt that this was an affront to the area and thus the evil spirit was sent forth to make her life a living hell.

As the spirit spoke through Cynthia, Debbie saw in her mind's eye a Native American spirit. This spirit was appeared as dark skinned and wore on its head a headdress of three feathers. On one side of the spirits head dress were horns like those of buffaloes. It wore a breastplate of bones that seemed to have a medallion center. A buffalo skin girded its waist. Its face was dark and the eyes coal black, but it had two white stripes on either cheek. Its face showed disdain for everyone in the room. In one hand it held a staff that had the head of an eagle impaled on the end and in the other hand, a bag of some sort that it kept waving in John and the Elwards direction.

Larry continued to recite the prayers of deliverance and Cynthia began to speak in her own voice and ask the Native spirits for forgiveness for her act of disrespect, explaining that she was a young child at the time and that she meant no offense in her actions and neither had her parents in allowing it to happen. As the prayers continued the vision of the spirit began to fade and Cynthia began to take on a softer look about her face. Soon she exclaimed that she felt that the spirit had left her.

AUTHOR'S UPDATE:

Cynthia has kept in contact with John and since the prayer session has had no more trouble with spirits. She is embracing her new life free from the spirit.

ONE ALTAR TOO MANY

Renee peered out the window into the encroaching darkness as fear and trepidation washed over her like the ocean waves washing upon the shore. As the last glimmer of light fizzled out and was swallowed up by the vengeful darkness, she began to feel its presence once again, slowly yet methodically making its way towards its victim. It seemed to want to make sure that every aspect of light was snuffed out before it made its move toward Renee. It was a move so calculated and motivated that she could not retreat from it.

As the sunlight slowly dipped below the horizon and the day slowly bled into the night, the dim streetlights began to flicker on, trying to become a welcoming beacon to stave off the muddiness of the night. Quickly the shadows lengthened releasing their long tentacles as if searching for an unsuspecting victim to latch onto and claim as their own.

Renee peered out the window at the impinging darkness as fear and trepidation washed over her like ocean waves wash the shore. Just as the last glimmer of light fizzled out and all daylight was swallowed up by the vengeful darkness, she began to feel its presence once again... slowly methodically making its way towards its victim. It seemed to want to make sure that every aspect of light was snuffed out before it made its move toward her. A move so calculated and motivated that she could not retreat from it.

Over the years, once she had come to terms with what was going on in her life, she had adapted her life, her way of living, so that she could continue with a semblance of what her life once was. She had searched far and wide for some way to keep this inhuman monster at bay. Lately though, the measures she was using seemed to be a losing battle in the war against the many onslaughts of this beast. Finally, she hoped that she had found someone that could help her in her plight against her unseen foe.

John Zaffis had been in the paranormal business for over forty years. This is what Renee wanted. If anyone could help her, she felt it would be him. She put in a phone call and was rewarded when he picked up the phone on the second ring. He listened intently to what she was telling him, and he decided to meet with her in a few days. As always, he planned to take the Elwards with him, as he was sure that a priest's prayers and a psychic's intuition would be needed.

The three made the 6-hour trip to upstate New York the next day. John had a feeling that they should not hesitate too long to get started with this investigation. Renee's house was a modest two-story home on a cul du sac. The surrounding homes mirrored hers and seemed to boast of a post-world war splendor in a forgotten era.

Renee ushered her guests into her small, cramped living room. As they looked around, it was evident through the clutter and disarray of the room, that she was indeed experiencing some turmoil in her life. They were not sure if it was paranormal or lack of motivation, but they hoped to find out what was going on. Seeing their wondering stares around her living room, she began to tell her tale before John got a chance to ask any questions. "It began about two years ago..." she started. "I began to notice that there always seemed to be something that would go wrong. No matter what I tried to do, it would end up in a disaster. I know what you must be thinking. It's easier to blame this mess on an entity, something that is unseen, rather than on laziness or my inability to keep a house neat and clean."

John quickly interjected. "That's not what we were thinking."

Yet, Renee continued almost as if she had not heard him. "I have been searching for help in dealing what is happening in my house. I am usually met with a lot of skepticism in my quest. I have gone to church, many churches as a matter of fact, but once the clergy have gotten inside my home and have seen the mess, they suggested that I do not need spiritual help, that in fact, I am suffering from a psychotic episode. So, I had to take matters into my own hands and to pretty much do what I needed to do to stop what is going on here. And it worked for a while, but I don't know if the entity got complacent with my attempts of keeping it at bay, or if I did it thinking these things would eventually work out. But in the last two weeks, this thing, or whatever, has stepped up its attacks on me, and right now I am at my wits end as to what to do next. That is why I am asking you for help."

John asked, "Well...what other than the disarray of the house is happening here?"

She looked at the three before answering, almost as if what she was going to say next would sound incredulous to their ears. "Well," she began. "I have been seeing a lot of shadows. First, they seemed to be playing hide and seek with me, but lately they are becoming bolder and are coming up to me as I am sitting having my dinner. They are in my bedroom and are following me around this house." Nervously, she looked around as if searching for something or someone, before continuing. "I hear voices and muted whispers mostly, but I have heard my name being called as if to entice me to follow the voice. I have been touched and poked when I am asleep. Once it was so hard that it woke me up and I was not able to get back to sleep. I have had smells that occur in the oddest places, and I can find no cause or reason for them." Renee paused as if she were thinking as to what to say next.

John told her "These are all classic signs of the paranormal activity in somebody's life. If it's OK I would like Debbie to do a walkthrough of your house to see what she can pick up that might hide from you...would that be alright?"

Renee nodded and then cautioned, "Be incredibly careful in the back spare bedroom, because two days ago, I had a spontaneous fire in there, and all the electricity in that part of the house is out. I just left it as it was. I was afraid that if I tried to clean it up or to fix it, things would happen again. Sorry."

John and Larry decided to accompany Debbie just in case, as they did not know exactly what they would encounter in the back part of the house. Renee chose to stay in the living room and let the three do their "walk thru."

The first room they walked into was the kitchen. It was in a little better shape than the living room, but not by much. There was an underlying smell of garbage and spices. Debbie noted in the far corner a small table had been set up with what appeared to be bunches of basil, onions and garlic around some crystals and a small dish of water. To them, it almost looked like an altar, and the items were either being used as an offering or as protection in Renee's hope of warding off her unseen foe. They ventured farther into the house curious as to what they would find next.

The next room was what appeared to be Renee's office. It too was piled high with boxes and things haphazardly scattered throughout the room. Debbie noted to the others, "The energy in this room is very high. Maybe Renee spends a lot of time in here as that would explain it." There was a small folding table in the corner with some items that were placed upon it. She looked closely and said, "These are reiki symbols on these papers. There are symbols for distance healing as well as the symbol for emotional healing and this symbol here is a power symbol, and this last one is to draw out negative energy." Debbie is a reiki master and teacher and therefore has knowledge of what these symbols are and what they represent, but she had never seen them used on a makeshift altar before.

They continued their way, venturing deeper and deeper into the house. The next room was what appeared to be Renee's bedroom. Here the energy was palpable to all. This was where she let her guard down while she slept, so the energy was more intense, almost as if it were calculating its next move while she slept in hopes that it would gain control. Debbie walked around the massive bed, picking up subtle, almost hidden, energies and visions of it. She said, "Here is where the entity stands, waiting and watching for the right time to make its move. It comes from the closet and as soon as Renee is asleep, it creeps out into the room. It then seems to go around the house causing chaos in hopes of keeping any semblance of help from her."

Once again there was a makeshift altar in one corner. This one seemed to be dedicated to St Michael the Archangel. In the center was a picture of St Michael stepping on the head of Satan, who seemed to be in agony. St Michael was holding his sword over his head. There were also crosses, a bowl of holy water, salt and what appeared to be a Eucharistic host, and other religious cards. John said "Well, let us go to the next room and see what we see there. This has got my interest piqued!"

They went into the next room and all that was in there was a large bureau and a single chair. It appeared that this room was devoid of the chaos that was in the rest of the house. This puzzled the trio. On top of the bureau was what they thought to be another makeshift altar. On a mirror was a brown lump-like substance. John told the others this seemed to be hair, possibly human, that was wrapped around something. No one dared touch it as they did not know what it was. There were two pottery candle holders that were molded in the shape of a ram and a bull. Black candles were placed in the holes in the top of their heads. Alongside these two figurines were sigils, which are inscribed, or painted symbol considered to have magical power. There were four sigils, and although they did not know what they represented, they surmised that they were probably something to be used to ward off whatever it was that Renee felt was going on in her home.

Lastly, they made their way upstairs to the attic where they found haphazardly stacked boxes, and in the center stood another altar. This one was made entirely of witch's runes, which are like the regular Nordic runes, and used in divination. Having knowledge of these runes, Debbie was able to "read" the message that the runes spelled out. She said, "This rune here that looks like a Y is for a woman...I suppose it's Renee. The next one that looks like an arrow pointing up is for a man. Perhaps her husband? The next one that looks like four arrows pointing in four different directions symbolizes a crossroads. The next one is a star...maybe hoping for help from above. And lastly this one is the eye. It can represent the use of magical powers and ramping them up." Again, Debbie said, "This is totally crazy! There is a different altar in all rooms. Is she mixing too many different types of religion together and making things worse?" she wondered aloud.

John answered, "I am not sure what she is doing at this point, or what the ramifications of having all of these altars could do to affect the energy in this house." He continued, "Let's go downstairs and see what Renee has to say about all this!"

The three made their way into the room where she was waiting for them. John sat down in front of Renee, and looking directly at her he began, "We saw the different areas in the rooms with what appears to be altars. These altars represent many different spiritualties. Could you explain what you're hoping to achieve?"

Renee sighed and said, "Throughout the years I have consulted many people, professionals in dealing with these entities. These professionals suggested what I should use in fighting these beings. Some of my altars are the results of my 'research'. I just thought I should try anything, and just maybe, all things would work. But sadly, things have only gotten worse. So, I started making barricades out of boxes filled with things to protect myself. As you can see, I am desperate!"

John looked at Larry and said, "Well Reverend...I think the best thing to do is a house exorcism, what do you say?" He agreed and started putting on his vestments. He turned to Renee and said, "What we're going to do is say prayers throughout your home. I am not too sure of how they will affect the energy of the various altars. I hope you're alright with this."

Renee nodded her head "Go ahead...and please do whatever you have to!"

He took out his ritual and began praying in the living room. "Exorcizamos te omnis immunde spiritus," which translated into English means "We cast you out every unclean spirit!" As he walked methodically in a wide clockwise circle and prayed, he sprinkled holy water and placed exorcised salt in the four corners of each room. John and Debbie followed behind using incense in each room. Their hope was to create an environment that would help to dissipate any negative energy.

In Renee's bedroom, Larry once again started the prayers. The three heard a low growl that emanated from the closet behind them. As they turned around, the closet door burst open and a serpent like creature slowly slithered towards the three. He stepped forward loudly praying, "Exorcizamos te omnis immunde spiritus!" He kept repeating the prayers and sprinkled holy water at the creature. Slowly the apparition withdrew back into the closet and slowly faded until it completely vanished all together. The air felt lighter, just like the air after a summer thunderstorm. The energy was lighter and calmer than when they first arrived.

Debbie sighed, "I don't feel anything negative now and the energy feels wonderful.

"John said, "OK...let's go to Renee and see how she's doing."

They found Renee in the living room, clutching a Bible. She almost looked sheepishly and said, "I figured I might have to hold onto this, just in case!"

John explained to Renee what had transpired and what they had done. He added, "And I think it would be in your best interest to take down all altars. These items, though well intentioned, have absorbed a lot of negative energy, and they just may be a gateway for the demonic to return once again." Renee assured them she would. She thanked them as they packed up to leave.

The next day Renee called John and told him that she had removed the altars and had started getting rid of her many boxes. After a wonderful night of sleep, she wanted to keep the positive energy in her home.

AUTHOR'S UPDATE:

Six months after their visit to Renee's house John received an update from her. She states that she has gotten rid of all the altars and has also removed all the boxes that she had all over her house. Her home, she reports is clean and clutter free with no more negativity.

THE TEXAS ENTITY

Recently, two women from the Dallas-Fort Worth area of Texas contacted John because they were both experiencing the same kind of attack, and they believed it to be the same demon attacking them both.

These two women, Margo and Darlene, had been friends for many years and had traveled all over Central America. Shortly after their last trip to Central America, they began to experience strange and unexplained maladies. Margo's hair began to fall out, followed shortly by Darlene's. Soon, they noticed that their skin seemed to change from the smooth skin that they once had to almost a lizard like appearance. They both seemed to experience tremendous weight gains and losses in a short period of time. They sought out medical intervention, thinking that they might have picked up some illness from their trip. All medical tests came back inconclusive for any maladies.

Soon, they both began to hear strange voices in their heads telling them outlandish things claiming to be the word of God. These voices began to speak to both Margo and Darlene about the dangers in the world today. The voice continued to try and persuade them to believe that it was the way and the truth.

Margo was the one who had made the initial call to John. She said, "Mr. Zaffis, if these voices that both Darlene and I heard were in fact the voice of God, we would feel differently than we feel when it speaks to us. We would feel joyful, enlightened, but we feel sad and confused...dirty almost. We know this is not the voice of God." She went on to say, "Three days ago it began showing us visions. These visions are not Godlike in any way. They are repulsive and frightening. Then Darlene got on the phone and said crying, "Mr. Zaffis, John we need your help. Please come to Texas

John hung up the phone. In his gut he knew that these two women were right, and that what they were dealing with was not God, rather the complete opposite. They were dealing with a demon masquerading as God to sucker these two friends in. That is why he agreed to fly to Dallas along with the Elwards to see what they could do to help these two women.

The three left early to fly to the Dallas airport. John wondered aloud as to what might have precipitated this case since nothing Margo told him during the initial phone interview raised any red flags. As it so often happens in the paranormal, the cause may not be discovered until after the case is over. Maybe this would be one of them. Time would tell.

As soon as their plane was air born, Debbie began to "hear" advice from the demonic. The demonic strongly urged John and the Elwards to turn back, to forget that these two women had called, and if they did not turn back, then the plane with all two hundred people would crash to the ground. Debbie tried not to listen, and all seemed to stop until about thirty minutes before they were due to land in Dallas. Debbie began to get "visions." The area directly in front of her turned a brilliant shade of green, and soon on this area, she began to see words forming. These words were written backwards as if written in a mirror. As this all unfolded before her, she began to hear a name, "Hempborious". The demon said that was its name, and it had walked the earth during the times of the Hittites. The Hittites were a band of nomadic people during Jesus' time. Then in front of her, in that green area, she saw the letter S U S E J. She quickly realizing that it was Jesus written backwards. As the plane descended to the tarmac, the vision faded and everything returned to normal with no further incidents.

Margo was at the airport to meet the group, while Darlene had stayed home with an unbelievably bad headache and stomachache. She had been fine until a few minutes before they were to leave for the airport. It seemed to come out of nowhere and was so severe and debilitating that she could never have gone to the airport. It was only a short drive to the women's house, and upon arrival, all were greeted by a much-recovered Darlene. She said to group, "It was so strange! As soon as Margo drove off, I immediately felt better."

John said, "It sounds like the demon was trying to separate the two of you! Remember there is safety in numbers."

As usual, John wanted to do an initial "walk through" of the house with Debbie to see if there were any hot spots that needed to be addressed in addition to any spiritual needs of the two women. They felt increased levels of negative energy in Margo and Darlene's bedrooms, but that was to be expected. The bedroom is usually the place that people let their guard down, where they relax and sleep. John took note of that as he and Debbie rejoined Larry and the two women in their living room.

Larry had been explaining what they would be doing, he concluded by saying, "Remember this is just a prayer - an ancient prayer for healing. There is nothing to worry about. If you hear see or feel anything, please let John or Debbie or I know. I will continue to pray until there is a sign the demon has left."

As soon as Larry put on his vestments, he took out his ritual book and began to pray over the two women. Margo immediately became ill. Her head and stomach began to ache. Then, John and Debbie also became ill. John had a blinding headache that came on suddenly, while Debbie was experiencing sharp stabbing pains around her waist. Later, she would discover that she had numerous welts and marks on her stomach around her waist. These marks, which were very painful, seemed to encircle her waist from front to back. There was a small area on her right side, however, that was not affected. Then she began to "hear" a voice telling her that when these marks met, she would die. It was the same voice she had heard during the flight. Then, what sounded like scratching coming out from the walls in the living room, there was a voice that began as a low whisper, but soon became a loud voice that said, "Stop! Shut the fuck up! I am your God! There is no one before me!"

Debbie would later recall, "I began to see a vision of a dirt floor superimposed over the rug on the floor. This dirt floor had stone steps that had many entities sitting on them. It almost seemed to be some sort of auditorium and the stage was in the center of the dirt floor. To the left was an opening that looked like a huge cave. It seemed dark and menacing to me. Out of this opening stepped a creature. I could not see its face, as it was clothed in a brown hooded robe that hid its face. The robe went all the way to the dirt floor. The being turned towards me and raised its arm and pointed an old, knurled finger at me. The hand reminded me of a dried-up old mummy hand." She continued talking about her vision, "It was angry that Larry was praying over these two women. It raged and screamed at me to tell him to shut up."

The group would later find out that one of the women was seeing and hearing all of this too. The demon went on to explain to the assembled group that these prayers would do no good, as there was no God. It went on to explain that if the demonic had to listen to the nonsense that Larry was saying, then we in turn had to listen to them from "their book." It continued to rant and to scream for him to stop praying.

It demanded that we listen to it and to know who the true Lord was overall, and that it was Satan. As the demon said this Debbie saw movement in the opening of the cave she was seeing in her vision, she looked in that direction. There in the opening stood who she believed to be Satan. She recalled, "This being, Satan as it wished to be called, was over eight feet tall, its arms hung ape like to its knees. The head was covered with snake like protrusions that encircled around two large horns on either side of its forehead. Its eyes were mere slits that glowed a menacing red on either side of a pig like nose. The mouth was open in a snarl and dirty yellow sharp teeth were exposed. A snake like tongue flicked in an out of the mouth. The skin on the body seemed to be that of a lizard and there were these pustules that seemed to have a liquid that smelled and looked like excrement. Out of these pustules the robed demonic creature picked some of this liquid and tried to get the two women to taste it almost as if it were a communion host. When they refused it became enraged not understanding why they would take communion from their false God and not the "true" communion of its lord Satan. "

Audible screams and growling could be heard by everyone assembled for the prayers. The room seemed to be filled with many black shapes and many demonic voices all claiming that Satan was the true prince of the world, that there was no God. These entities continued with the voices and blasphemous words. Everyone seemed to be under attack.

(Above) Larry praying while John takes pictures for documentation.

Larry kept losing his place during prayers. Both women held hands as Larry continued to pray. Soon, everything became quiet. Debbie noted that her vision started to change. Satan had disappeared from the opening, and the entities seated around the auditorium were gone. The robed creature too had disappeared, and the dirt floor that had been its stage was now empty.

At that moment, everyone saw a large shadow that resembled a sting ray that seemed to leave them both at the same time. They felt that they were delivered. And both declared both that they felt hungry. They had been unable to eat a normal meal in a long time. The demon would allow them to eat what and when it wanted them to eat. Margo had existed on cigarettes and chocolate for weeks, and Darlene had existed on coffee and bread for weeks. Finally, they were truly hungry for a good healthy meal. They both noticed that their surroundings seemed sharper and brighter and much more beautiful than they had remembered. They both recounted on how everyday objects would seem out of focus and far away, almost like looking through the wrong end of a pair of binoculars. But now, everything was sharp and focused. They both knew that had been set free from any demonic influence. Margo turned to the three, "I know I speak for Darlene too when I say you three have saved us from a hellish existence."

John cautioned, "Like us all, you still have to watch for any attempt by the demonic to enter back into your lives again. They are always around looking for us to slip up so they can get back in!" After assuring their three guests, Margo and Darlene took them out of a celebratory dinner before returning them to the airport to catch their return flight back home.

AUTHOR'S UPDATE:

Margo and Darlene contacted John a few months after his and the Elwards trip to their home. Although they are ever vigilant about avoiding situations that might entice the demon back, one question remains. What caused this horrific case to begin with? Did they travel to the wrong place at the wrong time? Was a curse somehow placed upon them? Did they bring home a "cursed" object as a souvenir from one of their trips? John and the Elwards learned a long time ago they would never find all the answers when it came to the paranormal, but the cause of this case remains a baffling mystery to this very day. Fortunately, Margo and Darlene continue to be demon free in their lives and they plan on staying that way.

DEMONIC ACTIVITY AND CHILDREN

One might wonder why the demonic would go after a sweet innocent child and what could this child have done to create the ideal breeding ground for demonic activity in their young lives. Sometimes, the demonic is brought into a child's life by their parents. Their parents are practicing members of a satanic cult and these so-called parents have offered or promised their child to their lord Satan.

Sometimes children become victims of the demonic from generational curses. This is through no fault of their own, or even of their parents and grandparents. Rather, they are cursed because of some long-forgotten deed on another.

Still, other children fall victim to the demonic due to the location that they live in, and with their trusting and believing natures, they attract the unwanted attention of the demons.

But the saddest way that a child might experience demonic activity is through abuse. Why would a child, after suffering abuse either physical or sexual have to deal with the demonic? Shouldn't it be the perpetrator? According to the clergy involved with deliverance and exorcism ministry, sexual abuse is so traumatic that it creates a "wounded soul," thus making it vulnerable to an attack from the evil one. Also, it is believed that since the abuser is pure evil, and the demonic has more than likely already claimed the abuser, the child is an innocent victim and ripe picking for the demonic.

Because of the ages of these children, all names and places are kept confidential.

THE BAD LIFE

Not too long ago, the young mother of a 5-year-old son contacted John and the Elwards in hopes of finding some help with nightmares and other problems that her young child was having. The child had been to many psychiatrists and had multiple diagnoses as to what was causing this child so much distress.

The mother, Melissa, related to John, "About 2 years ago, when my son was 3, my father-in-law came into our child's life. My father-in-law had been estranged from the family for many years but had recently returned to the area claiming he wants to make up for lost time with his family. My father-in-law doted on our child, Jimmy, giving as much as possible in the way of gifts and love. My father-in-law, Peter, even went so far as to not want us to discipline Jimmy in any way."

Melissa continued, "During Peter's visits Jimmy would run around like a wild animal screaming and yelling pure hatred towards us. Peter would smile and would allow - even encourage - Jimmy to play with knives of all things! No matter what my husband, Tom, and I said to Peter, this continued. Soon, Jimmy told us that grandpa was teaching him things that grandpa said to never tell us. That it was a secret only between him and grandpa. Jimmy became more and more unruly and seemed only to answer to his grandfather. Peter, in effect, turned on Tom and me for any form of discipline that we attempted on Jimmy. Things began to get out of hand with Peter, and we began to look for a way to keep him away from our child. Tom said that his father had been absent most of his childhood and early life, so he had no idea that his father was like this."

Melissa took and deep breath and continued, "We both have to work during the day, and although Peter asked to watch Jimmy while we worked, we decided it would be best to have Jimmy attend a day care center close by our home."

John looked at Melissa and asked her, "What happened with Peter. He did not take this lightly...or did he?"

Melissa answered John, "We naturally prepared for a tirade from Peter, but strangely he just nodded his head, smiled weirdly, and left. And we haven't seen or heard from him since."

John looked surprised and gave the Elwards a sideward glance, as if subconsciously sending them both messages of "Oh oh...hold on, there is more to this story about the grandfather and this kid that's going to come out."

Melissa continued, "But when Jimmy started attending school, he began to develop many strange symptoms that would leave him in a catatonic state for days."

John interjected, "Were any of the other children in the class affected in the same way?"

"No, just Jimmy," said Melissa. "He's been in and out of the hospital quite often during the school year. And as you asked, we at first felt that since this was a daycare that had many children from all over, that, therefore, he had picked up such illnesses not associated with the average child. But the day care told them that not one of the other children had developed any one of these symptoms. One day, Peter came to the day care and picked up Jimmy. We had put him on a list for pickup only if we could not be there in person to get him. We never thought he would just show up out of the blue and take him. They two were gone for hours until finally he brought him home without any explanation as to where they had been. For us, this was the last straw. We forbade him from having any contact with Jimmy, and we notified the authorities, as well as the school, that he was not to be near our child."

"Around this same time," she continued, "Jimmy began to have nightmares about a being that called itself the 'Bad Life'. This being would show him many things about life and the bad things associated with it. It began to tell him that it owned his life and that he should be grateful for being chosen from so many other children on earth. When he told us about his imaginary friend one evening at dinner, I was shocked. I turned and looked at my husband to see his reaction. At first, he had a blank look on his face, as parents sometimes do when a child comes up with an imaginary friend. But later, he took it more seriously. This thing or being also told Jimmy that it wanted to do away with his parents as they were in the way of him having a "gifted" life that only the Bad Life could give him once his parents were gone. The Bad Life would show Jimmy during the nightmares, how at one time it was an angel in heaven, but that this angel had been kicked out of heaven for being bad and had been sent to hell as punishment."

John let out a breath when he heard this. He immediately knew exactly what they were dealing with but needed some more information first before he could render a diagnosis on the situation. He asked Melissa for some more information, as he felt that this was just the tip of the "proverbial" iceberg.

Melissa once again started, "At first the Bad Life only came to Jimmy while he was sleeping, but very soon he could see the Bad Life during school, on the school bus, while watching television and even while playing. It seemed that no matter where or what he was doing the being would show up. When the Bad Life would be contacting him, his eyes would get all glassy staring straight ahead with a frightened look on his face. During these episodes, no one could bring him out of it. We tried everything to get him out of these states. We first took him to the ER, thinking he was having an epileptic seizure, but after many tests, the doctors could find nothing wrong with him, so from there on out we never took him to the ER again. Instead, we stayed by him, telling him how much we loved him and waited until the episode was finished. Afterwards, he would not remember anything but would be extremely tired."

She looked at her three guests, waiting for them to doubt her story like so many others had done before. But she did not see any doubt in their faces as they listened. John leaned forward and said, "I know this is hard but please continue and bring us up to speed as to what is going on with him right now."

She nodded and said, "In kindergarten, the episodes with the Bad Life became more and more prevalent, and now his teacher has begun to notice the effect that it has had on him, as well as the other children in class. Also, during this time, he would fly into what the teacher described as 'fits of rage', where it seemed as if he were an animal in a cage trying to get out. Jimmy started to beat up on the other students in the class. Then the worse thing happened... He began to tell the teacher and classmates about the Bad Life and his nightmares, but not in a plea for help, but way more so in a boasting way. So that led to the school officials meeting with us and suggesting that we seek help for Jimmy with the school psychologist. We agreed, as we were afraid of having the authorities called if we refused. So, we sent Jimmy off to the psychologist. After the initial interview, the psychologist said that our child was schizophrenic and needed to be put on medication to alleviate the symptoms."

Melissa went on, "Both my husband and I were not happy with the findings of the psychologist, so we decided to get a second opinion. We took Jimmy to other psychiatrists in hopes of finding an answer to the bizarre behavior of our son. But with each new psychiatrist there came a different diagnosis and another new medication, and he actually got worse instead of better. "

"One psychiatrist," Melissa went on, "After Jimmy told him about the Bad Life and the story that it was an angel kicked out of heaven, felt that the child was imitating what was said at home and on the school bus and using it to act out aggressions towards the other students. My husband and I are not religious people, and we assured the doctor that we had never discussed angels with our child. Still, the psychiatrist was sure that Jimmy had heard about the descent of angels on the school bus or at home, possibly in a cartoon or some TV show. But being five years old, we found it hard to believe that other children the same age would be discussing the fall of the angels from heaven on the school bus or even at school. But of course, the psychiatrist denied that some being that calls itself the Bad Life was responsible for telling Jimmy these things."

Melissa looked tired as she continued. "One day not too long ago at school, He had an episode that was so violent it left him in a catatonic state that the teacher could not bring him out of, nor after calling us at work, they could not bring him out of it. Usually when he had had an episode at school, the teacher could call his name and he would snap right back, but this time was different. The episode had caused him to twitch and shake uncontrollably, and as it progressed, moans and grunts could be heard coming from him. Eventually, he slumped forward onto the desk and started foaming at the mouth. The teacher tried to get him to respond several times during the episode, but after he began to twitch and moan, the school nurse was called as well as the principal. They removed him to the nurse's office where they waited for us. By this time, he had stopped the violent twitching and shaking and had become silent. He still seemed to be in a catatonic state, staring straight ahead with glazed eyes that seemed fixed on something that remained unseen to everyone but him. This episode was so violent, and he remained so long in a catatonic state, that it required us to place our 5-year-old child in a mental hospital for a few weeks. Still, he continued to have the episodes that became more and more prevalent. He was placed on medication, and the hospital sent him home to be seen as an outpatient over the next couple of months."

John drew in a deep breath as he contemplated all that she had told them. Again, he asked her. "Okay...was there anything else?"

Melissa said: "Although we continued to give him his medication, we began to look for an alternative solution to his problem. With us not having a church that we attend, we began to search on the Internet in hopes of finding someone to help with our problem. This is how we found you all."

After she had finished, she looked at the three and asked, "Would you all like to meet Jimmy?" She called him to come into the living room and meet their guests. At first meeting Jimmy, he seemed to be a very bright child and very inquisitive. John explained why we were there, as his parents had not told him anything about their visit.

Debbie said to him "We are here to help you, Jimmy. We work with other children that need our help in dealing with the Bad Life." The child listened to what Debbie was telling him and seemed to be relieved to hear that they could help him get rid of the nightmare that had invaded his young life.

Melissa explained to the trio, "Since coming back from the hospital three weeks ago, Jimmy had not talked about the Bad Life. We do not know if it was because the Bad Life is hiding from us or if he is afraid to talk about it. But after last night, we feel that it has not left him because I witnessed an episode as he slept."

Melissa sighed as if defeated and continued. "I went into his room just after he had fallen asleep. I just wanted to look at my child and wonder what had happened to this sweet little boy. I could see in the dimly lit room that he was tossing and turning in his sleep. As I got nearer to the bed, he began to speak...not in a small child's voice but in a deep, gravelly voice that sent shivers through me as I bent towards the sleeping child".

Melissa continued, "The voice told me that it intended to have my child as its own and that no one could save him from its hellish grip. It went on to say that it would destroy anyone that got in its way: his mother and father or anyone who tried to help this child. I let out a startled gasp, and hearing me, Jimmy turned his head in the direction of where I was standing. Instead of seeing his face, in its place was a very demonic face that had sores that oozed puss. And where there was once the sweet mouth of a child was replaced by something that resembled a mouth with razor sharp teeth behind blue cracked lips. This frightened me so badly that I fled the room calling for Tom to come quickly into Jimmy's room. I guess Tom saw the state that I was in and ran into Jimmy's room. He said he was expecting to find the worse, but all he found was a sleeping child... no sign of the demonic face that had frightened me a few seconds before."

Melissa had told Tom all that had happened. He found it hard to believe, but he agreed with his wife that something was wrong with their only child... something much more than a mental disorder. He was glad that they were having John and the Elwards come to investigate.

After hearing this John wanted Larry to pray with the family immediately. He leaned down to Jimmy and told him, "If the Bad Life says anything to you during the prayers make sure to let us know...okay?" Jimmy sat on the couch next to his mother and Debbie. Rev. Larry quickly put on his priestly vestments and took out a prayer book and some holy water. He began to pray over the small child. Soon the child told Debbie that the Bad Life was growling and claiming that it would never leave, that it loved the small tyke. Debbie said, "'Jimmy...the Bad Life must leave, and you must tell it to go."

With a voice far beyond his young years, Jimmy yelled for the evil entity to leave him. "Jesus says go!!!" Soon all became quiet, and the Bad Life appeared to have left the child.

The parents, although admitting that they were not particularly religious, requested that Larry administer baptism for their son. Rev. Larry, being an ordained priest, was happy to do it since he does not get a chance to do very many baptisms in this line of work. And little Jimmy was just as excited as the priest to have it performed on him.

As he performed the baptism ceremony over him, all was quiet, but John cautioned both parents that although things seemed to be quiet now, "the entity could, in fact, return seeking to regain what it had lost. So don't get discouraged or think that the whole process hasn't worked."

John contacted Melissa and Tom a few days after arriving home. They had some good news and bad news for John. First the bad: the day after John and the Elwards left, things appeared to get worse for Jimmy. Fearful, they had him admitted to the ER and the ER had him transferred to the children's hospital psychiatric wing. There, they tried some new meds and Jimmy seemed better, so he was soon allowed to leave the hospital on a "day pass," and Melissa decided to take him out in public to see how Jimmy would handle being in a crowd.

She took him to a fast-food restaurant near the hospital. It was very crowded that day. It was so crowded that a man and woman seemed almost to have to sit on Melissa and Jimmy's lap as they ate their lunch. They struck up a conversation with Melissa for a while and then abruptly left. Then, Melissa noticed that her wallet was missing.

Frantic she told the manager everything about the hospital, the Bad Life, the exorcism, the couple, everything. There was not much that the manager could do but watch her "meltdown," so Melissa went back to sit with Jimmy. Melissa told John, "I don't know why I blurted out everything that's happened, but when I saw that my wallet was missing, I just couldn't stop myself!"

"A few minutes later, a man approached us as we still were sitting there and said he was a minister and that he had heard all that I had said. He told me that he would like to pray over Jimmy, right then and there in the middle of the fast-food place, which he did. After the prayer he slowly backed away, but there seemed to be a peace around Jimmy and around me that was truly indescribable. I looked up to thank him, but he was gone, like he literally vanished into thin air.

Melissa was able to take Jimmy home and she is happy to report that the Bad Life has not returned, and that Jimmy is doing well. The medications been discontinued, and he seems to be able to maintain a normal life as a normal child. A "Good Life", so to speak...

Melissa is convinced that the "minister" was an angel sent by God to help her child get rid of the last remnants of the Bad Life. Was she right? While we may never know for sure, this much we do; all angels are ministers, and sometimes ministers can be angels in disguise.

AUTHOR'S UPDATE:

Melissa recently contacted John and reports that Jimmy continues doing well. There is no sign of the Bad Life, and he no longer talks about it either. She feels that the Bad Life is indeed gone for good and that they now can have a "good life." Her father-in-law, Peter, has not entered back into their lives either. Both Melissa and Tom want to keep it that way also. They do not want the negativity that seems to surround them when Peter is around, and they do not want or need his bad influence around their son, Jimmy.

THE COOKIE MONSTER DEMON

A very distraught mother of two, Sarah, from Maryland contacted John a couple of months ago. Her youngest daughter, Megan, who is four years old, was telling her mother that a monster lived in her room. At first, Sarah did not give much thought to her daughter's story, knowing that some children will do anything to keep from going to bed. This is what she thought Megan was doing, because as soon as she would climb into bed with her parents' bed, she would be able to sleep and not have any more nightmares.

John asked the mother, "Does Megan tell you if the monster tells her things?"

Sarah said, "Some of the things that would take place. One day, it said that her Daddy's car would have a flat tire on the way to work. She was so upset by this that she ran screaming to our bed to tell us what the monster had said. But we did not give the monster too much thought until my husband Paul did indeed have a flat tire on the way to work the next morning."

Sarah continued telling John, "Strange things began to happen in our house: noises, things being moved, lights going on and off by themselves and the television turning channels on its own. Paul and I looked for all logical explanations as to what was occurring so that we could rule out a lot of these occurrences, but many we could not explain away."

John asked, "Is anyone else being affected by these occurrences?"

Sarah said, "Our son, PJ, is being awakened by something pinching him as he slept. Also, when he would come home from school he would find his fish on the floor out of the aquarium, even though there was a top on the tank. The top is latched onto the tank and is difficult to unlatch, so it is doubtful that Megan could have opened it. Plus, she does not go in his room when he is not there."

She continued, "Just last week was Megan's fourth birthday, and I wanted to do something special, so I had a costumed character come to the party, the character was the 'Cookie Monster'. She likes to watch the Cookie Monster on TV. But when she saw the character, she ran screaming from the room saying that the Cookie Monster was the one hurting her. She finally told us that the Cookie Monster wanted to hurt her mommy and daddy!"

John was concerned and asked, "Could we do a tour of your house? What we look for is areas of high energy, so we can focus our prayers in that area."

On their tour, they noticed that the upstairs areas seemed to have an extremely high energy level, especially in the child's bedroom. There, they found a little girl quietly playing in the corner of the room. Lying on the floor was a stuffed Cookie Monster doll. Debbie picked it up and quietly asked Megan if this was the Cookie Monster that was hurting her? Megan said in a tiny voice, "He wakes me up by pinching me, so I run to mommy and daddy, but the Cookie Monster said if I tell he'll hurt my mommy and my daddy! So, I'm afraid to tell them!"

Everyone could see the anguish and fear on the child's face. She was protecting her parents the best she could from this unseen foe! John and the Elwards were saddened by her remark; to imagine the terror this small child was being put through was very upsetting to them. They had seen many people go through negative attacks, and all were bad, but seeing a small child having to deal with it was something else in itself.

They immediately began the prayers over the little girl who sat very patiently during the ritual they told her that these prayers would get rid of the mean cookie monster. She seemed relieved.

They also prayed in the house, with Rev. Larry burning incense and sprinkling holy water throughout the house. As they made their way downstairs Sarah suddenly said, "Before we moved in here, the previous family that lived here had a lot of kids and many of them were teenagers. We were wondering if they had been into some sort of occult practices, as we found large differently colored candles hidden in the rafters in the attic, along with some books on ritualistic Magic. Not thinking much about it, and to be honest with you, we did not at that time believe in this sort of stuff, however, we have since changed our minds about it. Anyway, we kept the candles in case of an electrical outage, but we are now more than happy to get rid of them. Do you think that this Cookie Monster thing was conjured up a long time ago and was finally making itself known?"

John answered her, "We may never know why this entity chose this time to enter into your lives, but if those teenagers did do ritual things, then a doorway could have been opened. And even if they were just 'playing around,' as teenagers do with this stuff, a doorway still could have been opened. And your young daughter could have just been what this entity was looking for."

Sarah thanked the trio as they were packing up to make the trip back home. John promised as he always does to keep in touch.

AUTHOR'S UPDATE:

John heard from Sarah recently, and all seems to be going well. Megan does not fear going to bed alone anymore and she is not afraid of the Cookie Monster anymore.

THE FAITH OF A SMALL CHILD

A very distraught mother, Catherine, contacted John late last year about her then four-year-old little daughter, Carol.

Catherine relayed to John, "We recently moved into our home and things seemed fine. Everyone was adjusting to the move, at first. But my daughter, Carol, has been having trouble sleeping lately and claiming that there were ghosts coming into her room at night. She would see spirits that would come with, what appeared to be, dry leaves rustling around their feet. These spirits would swirl into her room doing a dance, which is how she described it to me and my husband, Kevin, as to how these ghosts would act. All the while, the scratching sound of the dry leaves would echo off the bedroom walls. This would scare her so much that she would sleep with the covers pulled tightly over her head. In the morning, her hair would be so matted from holding the covers so tightly over her head that I would have a difficult time trying to brush her hair."

John asked, "Catherine has anyone else witnessed any of these ghosts?"

She answered, "Both Kevin and I have stayed up with Carol in her room, but neither one of us saw anything, at first. One night as I stayed with her, I started to smell a strange odor, that of dry autumn leaves, even though it was a hot July night. I got up out of bed and went to the window to see if something outside was causing the smell, but just before I got there, a noise stopped me. It sounded like something being dragged on the hardwood floor, and it seemed coming from the direction of her closet. I looked, but at first, I did not see anything. One of the doors slowly opened, and I don't know if you'll believe this or not, Mr. Zaffis, but a pile of leaves, dead leaves, came swirling out as if a gust of wind caused them to swirl out of the closet."

"Catherine," John said. "Please, call me John. Please continue. What happened next?"

"Well," she continued, "I was so frightened that I scooped up Carol and bolted with her to my bedroom. There, I woke up Kevin, and he went into her bedroom. But once there, he found nothing out of the ordinary. Not a leaf to be found! But he believed me, so we began looking for help. We approached our minister from our local church, and although we are highly active in the church, going every Sunday and both my husband and I are on many boards, he was afraid he could not help us as he told us it was a 'Catholic thing!' So, we turned to the Internet, and we found you." Catherine paused.

"Well, Catherine, why don't you tell me your address and I'll get my team together. When children are involved, I like to get there immediately before things get worse," he told her. Catherine told him where they lived, and since it was not too far, John made plans to meet with them later in the day. He would be bringing the Elwards, as both would be needed in this case.

As the sun was setting, John and the Elwards pulled into the driveway and were promptly met by Catherine and Kevin. The trio was ushered into a very well-kept home. Once in the living room, they met little Carol. She was a slight child with very bright eyes. She greeted her guests with a bright smile, saying, "Mommy and Daddy says you're going to get rid of the ghosts,"

Debbie smiled as she bent down to the little girl and said, "Yes sweetie. We are going to do our best!"

The three did a brief walk thru and then set about praying in the many rooms, especially in Carol's room, making sure to take extra care with the closet area. Debbie felt an unusual feeling of heaviness in the child's room, some spirit energy that seemed to be from a long-ago era. Deb asked Catherine about the history of the house. She told her that the house was over 150 years old and had remained in the same family, the Tauntons, for that entire length of time. The Taunton family had a young daughter who had passed away from scarlet fever or something like that. When we moved in, we found a box in this closet with an antique doll in it. Carol was too young to play with an antique, so we took it to the attic."

97

John asked Kevin to get the doll to ascertain if there was any energy around it. John held the doll for a couple of seconds and then passed it to Debbie. She confirmed that there was energy from a little girl around the doll. Rev. Larry sprinkled some holy water and then some blessed salt on the doll, at the same time explaining to the family, "Salt is a natural way to eliminate unwanted energy, and is used in the making of holy water, so this should keep whatever entities are here at bay." Then he proceeded to bless all the rooms of the house.

While this was going on, Carol, whose parents thought it was a good idea for her to accompany them while they did the house blessing, stayed quiet as if taking it all in. She heard all the prayers that Rev Larry was saying. In one particular prayer he was invoking the Name of Jesus. After he had finished, she looked at him and asked, "Can I tell them Jesus says go?"

Rev. Larry said, "Of course you can." And to the rest he said, "Such a simple prayer, but one that comes from a pure heart and from the unquestioning faith of a child. Its prayers like these that work the best."

As with what the trio likes to do with kids, is to give them a spray bottle with holy water in it so they can use it as a weapon of their own against the spirits. Little Carol seemed eager to use the spray bottle and more at ease than when they had first arrived.

After the prayers and blessings were over, the three re-examined the doll but unfortunately Debbie found it holding onto its spirit attachment, but the house felt lighter. So, Kevin and Catherine asked John to take the doll with him, they did not want to take a chance that the spirit would come back again as long as the doll was in the house.

With that John and the Elwards left for their drive home, with John as usual telling the family to keep in touch.

(Above) The Victorian doll

Catherine called less than a week after their visit. She was pleased to report, "As a family each night, we would say prayers, and Carol would always say 'Jesus says go!' And each night, when the ghosts would come into her room, Carol would spray some of the holy water in and around the closet. Then, she would lay a cross down there, and in a loud voice, say, 'Jesus says go!' Since your visit and our nightly prayer ritual, Carol does not see any more spirits and does not sleep with the covers over her head anymore."

AUTHOR'S UPDATE:

John hears periodically from Catherine. It has been a while since their visit, but the family keeps up the prayer rituals every night, and she is happy to report that all is quiet and there are no more spirits are invading Carol's dreams.

SPIRIT COMMUNICATION

Photo by Dan LeRoy Productions, LLC | danleroyproductions.com

For thousands of years, the living has been trying to communicate with the spirit world and vice versa. Over the years many devices and methods have been employed in order to make this communication easier.

In the 1800's there was an upswing of spiritual communication. It was the "Age of Spiritualism" which flourished during the years between 1840 and 1920. It was, and still is, a religious movement based on the belief that the souls of the departed are alive but in a different realm and can reach out and communicate with the living, who in turn, are also able to initiate and receive communication from the departed. The belief in "reincarnation" and "spirit guides", popular in eastern cultures and religions, were introduced to the western world. This "communication" most often utilized a "Medium"... a person with the ability to contact the spirit world. Many lives were lost in the Civil War during this period and many people were eager to contact their deceased loved ones. Mediums were sought out to help with this task. Unfortunately, there were some fakes out there that pretended to make contact by means of elaborate props and costumed figures to con people into believing that they had made contact. Although there were many fake mediums trying to make a quick buck by deceiving gullible people, there were also honest mediums who had the real ability to contact the other side.

As the years went on, more devices were invented to talk with the dead. Some say even Thomas Edison was working on such an invention before he died. Even though mediums still flourished a new way to speak with the other side was coming to the forefront. These devices made it easy for almost everyone to have a "conversation" with the dead.

OUIJA BOARD

The most popular, and according to some, the most dangerous device used for communication is the Ouija board - a game board used to talk to the dead. They are also called "spirit boards" or "talking boards." It is a flat board with the numbers 0-9 and all the letters of the alphabet. It has the words "yes" and "no" at the top with the word "goodbye" on the bottom. The board uses a planchette, which is a small plastic or wooden plank in the shape of an upside-down heart. It has a glass or plastic circle in the top where a pin is inserted into it. Ouija is usually used with two or more people who place a finger on the planchette. Someone asks a question, and supposedly, a spirit or entity answers by using the energy of the people who have their fingers on the planchette to slide the planchette for the answer.

The Ouija was created and named on October 30th, 1890, by a businessman named Charles Kennard. Elijah Jefferson Bond sold a patent for a planchette. He and Kennard teamed up with a cabinetmaker named Ernest Christian Reich. They started producing the wooden boards. Soon, Kennard took full credit for the invention and cut out Reich. Angry, Bond sold his rights to a man named William Fold, who incidentally made a fortune from the boards.

The makers could not decide on a name to call the board, so they asked the board. The board responded with "Ouija," which the board said meant "good luck." At least for Fold it was. He claimed in 1920 that it made him a profit of over a million dollars.

John and the Elwards have investigated many people who have used the Ouija board and have opened a door into the other side. One "memorable" case involved a young couple who used an Ouija board, along with another family member.

Two people sat around the board, while another, a skeptic, sat on the side lines. The two using the board began asking questions, and the board would respond with appropriate answers. At one point, the name "Zozo" came out when asked who the entity was. (Zozo is a demonic entity that is associated with the Ouija board. It is claimed that Zozo can mimic the voices of dead loved ones to pull the user into a false sense of safety on using the board, this demonic entity has been known to possess Ouija board users.)

The skeptic of the group did not believe in what was happening with the board, so one of the groups said, "Zozo, can you please show her you are real?" Immediately, the skeptic was immersed in horrible pain and screamed out. Scared, the other two immediately stopped using the board. They managed to help her into bed, and in the morning, she felt fine. All the pain was gone. She went to wake the other two and found that one of them could not move. All he could do was to speak and blink his eyes. Frightened, they called an ambulance and rushed to the hospital. Once there, he began to manifest more symptoms. He began to shake like he was having seizures, had difficulty forming words, could not use his arms and legs, and his head thrashed back and forth. The hospital ran many tests, but all the tests came back negative. They could not find a cause for his symptoms.

The doctors finally diagnosed the young man as having "conversion disorder." This is a disorder in which a person may experience blindness, paralysis, or other symptoms affecting the nervous system that cannot be explained solely by a physical illness or injury. Symptoms usually began suddenly after a period of emotional or physical distress or a psychological conflict.

Distraught, the couple turned to the hospital chaplain, who came in to pray with them. The Chaplain placed his bible on the young man. Suddenly, the young man said it felt as electricity shot through his body, down his legs to his feet, out through his arms and into each finger. Once again, he was able to move his extremities and to feel once again. The doctors were sure it was a mental problem and wanted to keep him for a mental evaluation, but the young man said he wanted to go home.

Once home, the couple's landlord stopped by for a visit and asked how they were doing. They explained everything to him, and the landlord said, "I am sure my parish priest can help you. Let me call him right now."

The couple agreed and the landlord came back and told them to go to the church and the priest would be waiting for them.

A few minutes later, they pulled up in front of the parish and went inside to meet with the priest, but instead they encountered the bishop. He said to them, "I understand that you think you need an exorcism? Well, you do know that this exorcism is all Hollywood hype!? This is nonsense. The thing to do is to go home, read these pamphlets and stop this demonic and exorcism nonsense." And with that they were dismissed and sent home.

They did read the pamphlets, which explained the power of prayer, the sacraments, etc., but it did not help much, as he could still see and hear Zozo. An apparition of Zozo would seemingly hide behind the furniture in hopes of tripping the young woman, but the young man would see this and warn her, which caused Zozo to fly into a fit. The entity would threaten and inflict pain on the couple. Desperate, they searched the Internet and came across Central Maine Ghost Hunters, led by Dustin Marcia and his team.

Dustin and his team did a thorough interview with the couple and an investigation of their house, and they concluded that the couple was indeed experiencing paranormal problems. A quick call to John, who then referred the case to the Elwards, as John could not make it. Soon the Elwards were on the way to the young couple's house. Joining Dustin and the Elwards was Cory Heinzen, who would later go onto own the infamous house of the Conjuring movie fame, but more on that later.

The house was very oppressive, as what was to be expected under the circumstances. So, Dustin, Cory and the Elwards got right to work. John, on one of his frequent phones calls, before and right after their visit, had mentioned that he wanted the couple separated during the prayer ritual. Cory volunteered to stay with the young woman in the kitchen. There was also the young man's sister (who had been the third person that participated in using the board) and his mother.

First, Rev. Larry prayed over the young man. Debbie could hear the entity pleading with the young man to make the priest stop, but Larry continued. Soon the voice of the entity got quieter and quieter and soon stopped altogether. Debbie happened to glance in the kitchen where Cory was, and she noticed that he was motioning to her as he was having a problem with the young woman. She seemed to be having great difficulty standing and walking. Debbie went out to help Cory and found that the woman's legs had swelled up twice their normal size. They looked painful. She seemed to be having trouble walking and was leaning heavily on Cory. Debbie grabbed the other arm and together she and Cory managed to get the woman to the bed.

The woman lay moaning on the bed, complaining of pains in her legs and arms. She explained that she had a history of fibromyalgia, but her legs, which seemed to be getting larger every minute, had never swelled up like that. Nor did she ever have any medical conditions to cause swelling of the limbs. Debbie asked her to pray but the woman could not, all she could manage to say was "JEEE," when she tried to say Jesus.

Larry was just finishing up with the young man, who had grown quiet and said that the entity had left. Larry went into the other room to begin another ritual by blessing the young woman. She held tightly to Debbie and Dustin's hands, squeezing so tightly as to cause both extreme pain. It seemed that the entity was not going to let go of this couple easily, as it felt as if both their hands were breaking from the force of the young woman holding their hands. Eventually, her grip loosened and finally released, and she seemed to be slowly coming out of it. Larry then finished up by blessing the house.

No one except the young woman was baptized, and after the ordeal that they just witnessed, all requested to have Larry baptize them. He baptized the mother, the young man and his sister. Afterwards, they were cautioned not to play with the Ouija board ever again. The sister assured them that it would never happen again as she had returned the board to the store where she had purchased it. When told about what they had done with the Ouija board in a phone call after the investigation, John said, "Not a good idea, but what is done is done. We usually either bury the board in the ground with blessed salt and holy water sprinkled over it and then covered in dirt. We never break it or burn it as the energy in the board could retaliate against you."

It was noted that the feeling in the house improved greatly as did the energy of the young couple.

AUTHOR'S UPDATE:

A couple of years later and the young couple are doing well. There have been no more physical problems with the young man and neither one has touched an Ouija board since.

SPIRIT VISITATION

Another form of spirit communication is spirit visitations. This happens when the spirit visits their loved ones with a message, confirmation of an event in the family, or just reassurance. Because they are recognizable or known to the person being visited, they are classified as "apparitions" rather than "ghosts."

John had such spirit communication a few years back. He had just gotten home from work and was bringing a basket of clothes to the bedroom. He dumped the clothes on the bed and turned to walk out of the room, when he suddenly realized his mother was standing there. His mother had passed a while back. He stepped back into the room, but his mom had vanished. Two days later his father passed. John is sure his mom was there to give him a message about his father. He feels if he had realized it was his mom and had acknowledged it, she might have said something.

In 1978 Debbie's son, Bob, fell ten feet to a concrete floor at an inside playground when he was almost three. He was rushed to the hospital and found to have a fractured skull, bruising around the eye socket. The area around the eye socket had also been crushed and his eye was bulging. The doctors kept assessing his condition, fearing a concussion and brain bleeding. Debbie was not allowed stay with him, so she and her husband got a hotel room near the hospital. The next morning, when they were finally allowed to see their son, he was awake. His head, swollen and bruised, looked absolutely awful, yet the doctors said he was not in any pain. Debbie and her husband stayed with him throughout the morning until the doctors asked them to go out for lunch so their son could take a nap.

When Debbie and her then husband came back, their son was sitting up in bed excited to see his parents. He looked at Debbie and said, " Poppy was here!"

(Above) Bob and his grandmother and grandfather

Debbie looked at him, thinking he meant her father-in law, because her father had died just eighteen months previous. She said, "Oh no honey, Poppy Gillette is at work. He'll be here tonight."

But her son shook his head and adamantly said, "No your poppy! He was here he showed me his birdie on his arm." Debbie's father had a tattoo on his right forearm of an American eagle, and Bob used to trace it with his finger as he sat next to him. Bob went on to say, "He told me I was going to be alright and then he said goodbye!"

At first Debbie was frightened as she knew all the tales about how family members come to escort their loved ones across to the other side. She prayed that this was not the case. But two thirty-years later, she realized that her son was her father's first grandchild and that he had told Debbie the night before he died that he would always watch out for Bob. Debbie's dad was right. Today her son is fine a grown man with a family of his own.

Rev. Larry did not have this visitation communication but rather Debbie's daughter did. They had been struck by a car as pedestrians one April morning in 2003. It occurred the night after the accident. Debbie had been discharged from the hospital and was back home. Her kids were there helping her. Rev Larry was in the hospital seriously injured, barely clinging to life. A 20% chance of survival was what the doctors were saying. While Debbie was getting periodic updates from his doctors, her children were sleeping in the living room. Debbie's daughter, Stacey, got up to check on Debbie, and she encountered Larry's mom, who had passed four years before. Stacey said quietly to the apparition, "He's in the hospital." With that, the entity faded.

Even famous people from history have had spirit visitations. When President Abraham Lincoln was getting ready to travel from his home to his inauguration, he saw an apparition of himself standing beside him in the mirror. This vision was of a much older, more tired Abraham Lincoln. His wife, Mary, who herself was a great believer in "spiritism" and "séances," upon hearing of her husband's encounter with the spectral visitor, surmised that he would have a full first term, but that his second term would be cut short, which it was. Shortly before his assassination, Lincoln was awakened by the sound of someone crying. He got out of bed and followed the sound. He followed the sound to the East Room and was surprised to find soldiers standing at attention around a flag draped coffin. Walking up to the first soldier Lincoln asked, "Who is dead in the White House?" The soldier replied, "The president of the United States!" Lincoln was a shocked to see a likeness of himself lying in the coffin.

Another visitor to the White House was Queen Victoria. She was awakened by someone knocking on her bedroom door. Upon opening it, she saw the specter of Abraham Lincoln standing there. Slowly, he faded away.

Hillary Clinton remarked one time that she felt Eleanor Roosevelt's presence when she and Bill lived in the White House. Unfortunately, she was ridiculed for talking with a ghost.

Even Harry Truman reported that on one occasion heard a knocking on his bedroom door. He jumped up from bed and opened the door and found no one there. Thinking that maybe it was his wife or daughter, he checked on them and found them sleeping safely in their rooms. Where upon, President Truman remarked, "Well, I guess this place is haunted."

Annie Surratt is the daughter of Mary Surratt, who was convicted of playing a role in the Lincoln assassination. Many have sworn that the ghost of the young Surratt is seen knocking at the White House's front door, begging to have her mother released. Unfortunately, Mary Surratt was found guilty and hanged.

Still there are reports of Abagail Adams being seen in the East Room where she used to dry her bed sheets. She is seen with her arms outstretched as if she were carrying the bed sheets in from the line.

President Woodrow Wilson staff would report of seeing Dolly Madison enjoying her favorite eternal pastime of taking care of the Rose Garden.

All throughout history, creditable people have reported spirit visitations. Many visitations have occurred during times of trouble. Many are given warnings or messages, and still many others are comforting just knowing that love does not end at the grave, but rather it continues long after.

AUTHOR'S UPDATE:

Debbie's son still is doing well. He has not seen his poppy since that time, but even after all that time he vividly remembers his "visit."

Larry has recovered from the horrific accident and there have been no more reported visits from his mother.

John is sure that his mom did visit just before his dad died. Whether she was there waiting for his dad or giving John a message, he will never know. But either way, the three are comforted by their love from beyond the grave.

EVP

Electronic voice phenomenon, or EVP, is used widely by paranormal investigators. A recorder, usually tape or digital, is set up and questions are asked. Most times, there is an answer that is not heard audibly, but is heard later on the play back. New and improved devices, some quite costly, seem to appear on the paranormal market almost on a regular basis. Lately, with cell phones making our lives easier, and this includes paranormal investigations too, there are many phone apps available that make EVP recordings more accessible and convenient, especially for the amateur ghost hunter.

John, Larry and Debbie have used these apps on a lot of their investigations, sometimes with amazing results. Lately their old mentor and John's Uncle, Ed Warren, has been very vocal on their investigations. Ed, always the jokester, will often tease the three of them. He will offer insight into their investigation, and many times will give them messages that will only pertain to the three of them. It is always an interesting "conversation" with Ed, as a few of the messages are in riddle like form and they must figure out for themselves what exactly he is trying to convey. The strange thing is that when the voice comes over it, is Ed's voice, no doubt about that. Larry tends to stay clear of EVP sessions because he claims to be unable to make out the words many times. But when Ed Warren comes through, he says he comes through loud and clear. "There's no mistaking that voice" he says. The voice talks in the same manner and tone Ed used.

The first time they heard Ed's voice, John had asked, "Are there any spirits here?"

Spirit answered, "Yes."

John asked, "What is your name?"

Spirit answered, "Ed."

John looked at Debbie and Larry and said, "Oh my God, do you guys recognize that voice? Ed is that you? What do you want?"

Ed said, "Yes, it is me! I am a ghost!"

(Above) John and his Uncle, Ed Warren

It appears that Ed has joined his beloved nephew as well as the Elwards on many of their investigations. Recently, Ed joined the three on impromptu investigation into a supposedly haunted house in Mystic, Connecticut. This area of the state has always a favorite place of the Warrens and to John as well. It is steeped in history and boasts a Seaport village that has been recreated to look exactly like that of a 19-century fishing village. Many of the 60 buildings that were moved there were restored so as to appear similar to as they were when they were new. It is a very active tourist location. And so, it seemed fitting that Ed would make his presence known to the assembled group.

As the group settled into the dining room, much paranormal equipment was set up and hopes ran high for some information to come forth from unknown spirits. Soon, the ghost equipment began to come alive as many entities began to come forth. Everyone was mesmerized as the lights on the equipment blinked on and off, while sounds came from the numerous gadgets that the paranormal enthusiasts had placed around the room. Soon, a much-recognized voice burst forth from the ghost meter and was immediately recognized as Ed Warren by many of those present who had known him in life. Ed had brought with him many spirits that wanted a chance to communicate their story about their life and death. And Ed, never quiet, soon began to tell his story as well...information that he wanted people to know that had long since been kept in the dark. John and the Elwards were perhaps surprised but were not shocked to have many questions answered by Ed.

Ed is not the only entity that has come through whose voice is recognizable. Debbie and Larry's family members have also come through, many times brought through by the courtesy Ed Warren himself. It seems that even in death he is still very much the paranormal investigator.

Recently the trio did some EVPs in a local cemetery. They were rewarded with the voices of many spirits that were buried there, as well as once again hearing from their mentor, Ed Warren. And this time, Ed brought forth Lorraine, who of course was known to all three. Lorraine, also never a quiet one when it came to getting her message across, acknowledged the three and began to say some things. There were things mentioned that that only the three would understand and were as enlightening to them as when Ed had spoken to them in Mystic.

AUTHOR'S UPDATE:

Ed has communicated with the three. They have all felt his presence many times. Debbie and John have seen him a few times, as well. He is, as always, ready to help on an investigation... just as he did in life. Lorraine too continues to offer her insights as well.

John and the Elwards as well as other paranormal investigators continue capturing EVPs with astonishing results.

Remember that the dead DO tell tales... so listen carefully!

BUYER BEWARE

Photo by Dan LeRoy Productions, LLC | danleroyproductions.com

Who does not like to find a good deal? Perhaps a must needed item, or a remembrance of time gone past. Many people love to shop at thrift stores or flea markets or at local tag and garage sales. There is a saying that "one man's trash is another person's treasure," but is that really the case? Sometime those "must have" items could hold onto a nefarious intent on the unsuspecting person.

John has helped many individuals to eliminate unwanted items from their homes. Along with the Elwards, he has traveled extensively to aid people who discovered that their much-needed remembrance item held more than just a fond memory it harbored an entity that only had the urge to humiliate or harm an individual.

Many times, he will receive packages from people all over that think they have gotten a "treasure," but what they have is a nightmare waiting to unleash its wrath on the unsuspecting. On the following pages John and the Elwards have compiled a few cases of when the buyer should have been more aware of what they were purchasing.

THE KETTLE OF CALAMATY

John was just finishing up with cataloguing his huge collection of haunted dolls when the phone rang in his adjacent office. Picking up the phone on the second ring, he heard a very haggard sounding voice ask, "Are you still collecting haunted items?"

John answered hesitantly, "Yes, I am, but could you please give me some background as to what is going on, what the item is and why you think it's haunted? And could you please start with your name, please?"

The woman on the other end seemed to take a deep breath and began once again, "Oh I am sorry I am just so upset. I just did not think. My name is Florence, and I got your name and number on the Internet. I waited as long as I could to call you. I will start at the beginning and tell you what has been going on. First, my mother recently passed away."

John interrupted her, "So sorry, Florence."

She continued, "Thank you. She had been sick for a while, and my sister, brother and I knew that it would not be long. My mother was the kind of woman that kept to herself, and all though we loved her dearly, I am ashamed to say we rarely saw her at her home. Instead, we only saw her at my house or my sister or brothers' houses. We never really gave it too much thought until after her passing.

"Well John, our mother was a hoarder," she continued. "We found that out when we went to her house after the funeral. My siblings and I were at a loss as to what we saw! The windows had all been cardboard over. The smell that emanated from the house, even before we opened the door, was gagging. That should have prepared us for what we encountered upon opening the door, but no, it was far worse than we could have imagined. Garbage, papers, clothes, food items and waste products were piled haphazardly around each room.

"As we got deeper and deeper into the hoard, things became worse. I honestly do not know how my mother lived like this and still managed to function outside the house. But that is not why I contacted you.

"As you can imagine with all the things in that house, there were some strange things that she had. We think that mom just picked up things from the side of the road or the garbage - wherever she saw something that might feed her disease of hoarding. We did not save much but some of the more unusual items we did. And I think that is where the problem came from."

John gently guided the woman to continue, he knew that she was in a fragile state having just lost her mother and finding out that the woman lived in squalor was horrible. "Florence what strange things did your mother have?"

She seemed to be calming down under his gentle manner of speaking. "At first neither my brother, sister or I didn't think too much about this kettle. It was cast iron and very heavy and in surprisingly good shape. My brother, Ted, was the first to take it. He thought it would be a good kettle for camping, as he does a lot of it.

"On the first camping trip, Ted said strange things began to happen in his house. As he and his wife loaded up the camping gear, things they placed in the camper would be gone when it was time to unpack, and of course this caused a lot of tension between them, each accusing the other of leaving the times behind. Other things happened as well.

"The plumbing in the camper backed up even before they used it, the grill on the stove did not light and finally they left early. On the way home, their camper overheated and had a flat tire. Ted has a bit of a suspicious nature and has read up on these weird things. Somehow, he put two and two together and figured that maybe it was the kettle since that was the only new item that he had. So, he was telling my sister, Chris, and I all about it.

"Now, Chris is a non-believer in the supernatural, and she laughed at Ted and said that she would take the kettle. A few days later my doorbell rang, and it was a very ashen faced Chris. In her hands was the kettle. She literally dropped it at my door and left, saying very little. Only, "Take it I do not want it in my house," and then she left.

She paused in her narration, and John took this opportunity to ask her gently, "What happened next and what did you do with the kettle?"

She seemed to heave a deep soulful sigh as she continued, "Well I did not think too much of the kettle, so I picked it up and put it in my garage, and I went back into the house. A few short hours later I heard what could only be described as pure horror. The noise coming from my garage was horrible. It sounded like an animal was being tortured and was in its death agony. The screaming, the smashing sounds - it sounded like all hell was breaking loose in the garage.

"I ran to the building, thinking that surely the neighbors were hearing this bedlam and would be calling the police. I opened the door and expecting to see complete devastation. I saw nothing. Nothing was out of place, and everything was just as I had left it when I placed that cursed kettle there. As I picked up the kettle and I began to examine it, I noticed that there was residual in the bottom as if something had been burnt in the kettle. I highly doubt it was used for tea. This made me wonder if my brother and his wife had examined the kettle or if they were waiting to use it while camping. Anyhow I got a box and placed the kettle in it. As I did, I noticed that there were stars around the top of the lid. Now, I am not sure, but I think that has something to do with witchcraft, so I sent you the kettle and you should be receiving it in a few days. My siblings and I are glad to be rid of it and are sure you will know what to do."

He told her that he would call her when he received the package. Many times, people will send items to John before speaking with him as Florence did. He will just receive the items with stories about how they were acquired and nothing more.

A few days later a package did arrive, and John opened it, as he does all packages, in an adjacent area from his house and museum. He likes to give them what he calls some "breathing room" until he can place them in his museum. The kettle was no exception.

He examined the cast iron kettle. It was very heavy and in great condition. The lid had five pentagrams around it. All in all, the kettle had extraordinarily little rust or dents on it, but there was some kind of muck in the bottom that looked like it had been used to burn something.

(Above) The kettle of calamity

He knew that there could be any number of things that could have been burned in the kettle, and there could also be any number of reasons that these items were burnt. He also knew that he would probably never know the exact reason the kettle was used for, and he thought it was best to safely place the kettle in his museum and make sure it was left alone.

He called Florence, as promised, and told her what he felt. She was glad to have the kettle out of her and her sibling's lives. She promised if anything more happened, she would reach out to him immediately.

AUTHOR'S UPDATE:

John has heard nothing from Florence or her brother or sister, and repeated calls to her number have gone unreturned. John can only hope that no news is good news.

THE PICTURE

The allure of American primitive art seems to call to many people. It is a testament to a bygone era, specifically the early to mid-19th century, when photography was not yet invented and painted portraits of family members was a way of remembrance. It is not strange to find that even today, many years later, primitive art is still popular.

Beverly, a collector of this type of art, found that she got more than she bargained for when she bought a framed picture of a young boy and his dog. She should have been a little suspicious when the price of the large painting was only a few dollars at a local flea market, but she was so excited to be able to purchase the item that she did not give it a second thought. She brought the painting home and hung it in a prominent place in her living room. There she could admire it as she was extremely proud of that picture.

A short while after purchasing the picture, a neighbor came in and Beverly proudly showed off her latest acquisition. The neighbor looked at the primitive and said, "Why in Heaven's name did you buy that picture? It is awful it should not be in this house. If I were you, I would get rid of it immediately."

Beverly laughed and said, "But I love this picture and I think its fine."

Shortly after the visit, she woke up one morning and found everything in her living room scattered about. Tables and chairs were upside down, and it looked as if a huge brawl had broken out. And yet she did not hear a thing. She thought to herself, "What is going on?" She readied the room back the way it was and then went about her day. She did not really give it too much thought until the next day, and then the day after that, when it happened again!

Everything was upended in the room, but now other things were happening too. She started to "lose" things. She would place them down and then go to retrieve them, but they would be gone, only to be found in a completely different place or most times not at all. She began to hear her name called out in a seemingly empty room by a small male child. Perplexed, the woman began to do research online as to what might be happening in her home. Many articles intimated to it being the start of a haunting and with those articles she kept seeing the name John Zaffis. She then contacted him and asked him as to what might be going on in her home.

He agreed to go to her home to assess the situation. Since she did not live too far from him, he asked the Elwards to join him in the investigation. They made the trip later that day.

Upon entering Beverly's comfortable home, Debbie was immediately drawn to the picture. She picked up that there was a spirit associated with it. John did not tell Debbie anything about what the woman claimed was going on in her home so she could independently verify the homeowner's claims. Debbie discerned the spirit of a small child. He was sort of a spoiled little boy who was used to getting his way when he was alive and was even more so now that he had passed. He had attached himself to the picture his parents had commissioned after his passing from scarlet fever. They had his dog Prince sketched into the painting, as well. Prince was apparently a favorite pet of the young lad. Somehow, over the years, the young boy's ghost had gotten lost along the way, as spirits sometimes do. He just recently had made his presence known when the woman purchased the picture. Perhaps he was attracted to her aura, her presence or because she lovingly took care of the picture... whatever it was that had awakened his presence.

After hearing what Debbie had picked up regarding the painting Beverly, despite her affection for the piece, no longer wanted it in her home or anywhere else for that matter. She asked John to remove it. He agreed, but as a safety measure, suggested Larry do a house blessing to make sure everything would remain quiet.

The three departed for home, and upon arriving, John placed the large picture in his shed until he could get it to his museum. He and the Elwards went upstairs to recap the case. Suddenly, they heard a crashing sound that came from the shed. They ran to the shed and found that the picture had flown across the room and was now on its side facing in the opposite direction from where John had placed it. It seemed as if the boy in the painting was having one last tantrum for himself.

The next morning Beverly called John again to report that nothing had happened in her home. All was quiet, and nothing was thrown about. It seemed that removing the picture did the trick. She told him that from now on she is going to be careful as to what she buys, because sometimes a good bargain is too costly.

AUTHOR'S UPDATE:

John has heard from Beverly. She reports that her house is quiet and she has stopped going to flea markets to pick up random items. She does not want a repeat.

UNMASKING EVIL

The word mask first appeared in the English language around the 1530s. It was derived from the Italian "Maschera" from the Medieval Latin word "masca", and it means a covering to hide or guard ones face.

The use of masks in rituals and or ceremonies is a very ancient practice across the world. Masks can also be worn for protection, hunting, sports, feasts, in wars, or simply for ornamentation. Many people collect masks for this purpose, as these ceremonial or decorative masks were not designed to be worn. Although the religious use of masks has waned, masks are used sometimes in drama therapy or psychotherapy. And they are especially used during the Halloween season.

Clarisse always loved masks. She found them beautiful to look at. All the intricate designs and many colors always held a fascination for her. She found just looking at them could lull her into a sense of euphoria unlike anything she had ever experienced before. So, when a local estate sale had a collection of masks for sale, Clarisse jumped at the chance to make them her own.

The day of the estate sale dawned grey and overcast, but Clarisse's spirit was not at dampened by the weather. On the contrary, she felt ecstatic about going on the hunt for the perfect item. On a table upstairs in the home Clarisse saw what she had sought - ten beautiful wall masks. They were not old, but they certainly were not brand new.

To her, each one seemed to depict a different mood or emotion. One was of a circus clown. It seemed to depict a gentler time and gave off an emotion of happiness, while still another one depicted sadness, giving Clarisse a feeling of hopelessness. Another one brought out a feeling of loneliness. Each one seemed to call out for her, so she made the purchase. She was anxious to get home with her treasures and hang them in a prominent place in her home. She wanted everyone who would visit to marvel at their exquisiteness. She was absolutely enchanted and seemingly spell bound by them.

But alas, her hopes were dashed as things did not go as planned. A few of her friends thought that the masks were creepy looking. Rather than giving off the warm fuzzies, they gave off feelings of dread and even fear. Clarisse could not understand it, but a quick trip out of town soon showed her what others were feeling regarding her masks.

Upon returning to her home, Clarisse was surprised to find that, instead of a welcoming feeling, she was filled with anxiety and despair in her once comforting home. She could not understand this feeling. The home where she once found joy seemed to have vanished. Things seemed off and she could not understand what was going on.

She confided to her best friend, Margo, about these feelings, and the friend suggested that perhaps it had something to do with an item she had recently purchased. Margo, who was a firm believer in the paranormal told her, "I just watched a show about people that buy things not suspecting that these items have a nefarious agenda in their new owners lives. There is a man and his team that will come and remove these items. His name is John Zaffis, and he is local. I think you should give him a call before things get bad. If it is nothing, then you will feel better."

Later that day, the phone in John's office rang while he was putting the finishing touches on his latest presentation for an event he was doing. Clarisse felt immediately put at ease by his charismatic way of talking. She explained what was going on with the masks and what her friend had said.

He said," Yes, your friend was correct about haunted items. Some things just seem to harbor negative energy. When they are mixed with an unsuspecting person's energy, they can really disrupt their lives. What you are telling me is that there is a possibility that the masks are the reason that you are feeling like you do in your home. My team and I can come to you home and see what is going on. I will be bringing a psychic so that she can discern what is going on as well as a priest who can bless your house and return some balance to your life once again."

A short time later, John and the Elwards were pulling up to Clarisse's tiny one-story home. The home was cozy enough, but Debbie felt an anxiousness upon entering. It was as if there was something lurking in the shadows just waiting and watching. She began her walk through as the other two sat speaking with Clarisse.

(Above) Debbie and Larry examine the masks

The first room she walked into appeared to be Clarisse's study, and on the walls hung her prized masks. She took a closer look at them and discerned a subtle ancient energy that emanated from the masks. Puzzled, she looked closer at the masks. They did not seem all that old, and she did not understand why she was feeling this type of energy from them.

Finishing her walk-through, she joined her teammates and Clarisse in the living room. John was the first to speak, "Well, what did you discern?"

Debbie sat facing the rest and began, "I did not feel anything until I entered your study, Clarisse. The masks on your wall seem to give off an energy that I cannot explain. The masks are fairly new, but the energy has an ancient feeling to it. I do not feel it has gotten too far in whatever it planned to do concerning you, so I feel that perhaps we have caught it in time."

John turned to Larry, "I would like you to start in this room. Go throughout the house saying prayers and then conclude in the study where those masks are hung."

Larry began the prayer, "Lord, we beg you to visit this house and all who dwell in it." He moved clockwise throughout the rooms, ending up in the study. There he began the prayer as he stepped closer to the masks. Suddenly, one of the masks flew off the wall, hitting him in the forehead. It gave him a small cut over his left eye, but he, nevertheless, kept praying. Luckily, the cut was just a superficial one.

Everyone was shocked, especially Clarisse. She said, "Up until this moment, I did not really feel that there was anything wrong with the masks, but now I know there is! Larry I am so sorry this happened. John, please take these masks. I do not want them in my home! I do not trust what might happen if they stay. "

John and the Elwards boxed up the masks and took them home. John, after putting them in the sun light, as he does with many of the haunted items he receives, hung them in his museum.

AUTHOR'S UPDATE:

Clarisse has kept in touch with John over the course of a few months. She was concerned about Larry's injury but was relieved that it was not more serious. She reports that all her feelings of anxiety and despair have disappeared, and she is enjoying her home once more.

I DREAM OF JINN

Genie, or Djinn, are supernatural beings that have been written about in early pre–Islamic Arabian mythology and theology. They have a broader meaning of demon. Jinns, djinn or genie are not just an Islamic concept, as they may represent several pagan beliefs as well. Djinns are thought to cause hardships, misfortune, diseases and possessions. They are neither human nor angelic, and can appear in many forms. To get rid of a djinn, one must purify their lives and thus make their spiritual shield strong.

Dhar Omar was a thirty-something CEO of an up-and-coming software company in Levelland, Texas. Over the last few years, Dhar had developed a way of competing with the more notable software companies, and thus, had drastically cut the competition down to a more manageable size. His fluid approach to his competitors was widely known throughout Texas, and soon, if he had his way, so would the rest of the country. But Dhar's success seemed to come at a cost, at least with his personal life. He had recently ended another romantic relationship. His relationships never seemed to last long, no matter what or why. It seemed like he was a wiz in the software company, but he seemed to fail in his personal life.

As Dhar walked through his spacious condo, he glanced around at his many works d'art that he had acquired over the years. He had become quite enthralled with his recent acquisitions from the Middle East. One, in particular, was his favorite. It was a bust of a man wearing a tan turban. The young woman who had accompanied him on that trip had laughed and called the statue "Dhar Tifl," which means "baby Dhar." Throughout the trip, the woman kept referring to the statue as Dhar Tifil. Shortly after returning from the Middle East, the relationship ended leaving Dhar alone.

(Above) The statue

He thought about this as he walked through his lonely rooms. What was wrong with his life? He had always tried to live a good clean life, but lately it seemed as if he was just stuck in a rut. Dhar's brother had come for a visit recently and had told Dhar that the statue made him feel strange and angry. It was as if the statue was emitting some sort of energy of jealousy, as if it wanted to keep Dhar all to itself. The brother told Dhar that he should get rid of the cursed item and get a holy man into cleanse the place.

Although Dhar thought his brother was a bit strange to suggest such a thing, he began to wonder if his brother was right. So Dhar began a search of a Muslim Imam that had experience with Djinn, since that is what his brother had suggested was residing in the statue. And then he needed someone to take the statue and keep it safe from anyone else who might come in touch with the energy.

The first name he came across was John Zaffis. Dhar noticed that John had an extensive knowledge of many religions, as well as a network of clergy from all denominations scattered about the country, as well as the world. He immediately contacted John, who made the young man feel at ease. Dhar told him what his brother had told him and about what had been going on in his life.

John said, "You know, Dhar, I believe what you brother suggested. It is possible the statue has some energy around it. By you and the young woman giving it recognition, it might have woken something up. I can suggest an Imam that I know who resides in Lubbock, Texas. It's not too far from you. I will make a call and get back to you as soon as I speak with him."

John hung up and called his associate to set up a visit with Dhar. The very next day, John's associate, an Imam from Lubbock Masjid or Mosque, as we would call it, arrived at Dhar's home. There, he recited the ancient prayers of deliverance, while reading from the Quran, as well as other prayers. All was quiet while the prayers were said. The Imam and Dhar boxed up the statue and sent it to John, who had agreed to store the statue safely away from anyone coming in contact with its energy.

AUTHOR'S UPDATE:

John recently talked and Dhar and reports that things are looking up for the CEO. He has recently met a young woman and things appear to be going well for them as his business continues to do well.

HAUNTED LOCALES

Photo by Dan LeRoy Productions, LLC | danleroyproductions.com

THE FARM

There are many well-known houses around the world: the White House, The Winchester Mystery House, Graceland and even Buckingham Palace. All these places of residence are unique, yet they all have one thing in common. They were occupied by people who lived, loved and grew. A house is not just a wooden or stone structure. It is more like a place for dreams to grow. Sometimes these dreams will become nightmares in some houses, like the case of the Winchester Mystery House where a widow feared the spirits so much that she kept building onto that house right up until her passing. There is another house that holds secrets so deep and dark, they have caused the spirits not to be at peace. This house is known as the Farm at Round Top Road, or as it is notoriously known as "The Conjuring" house of Hollywood fame.

This quaint farmhouse did not start out to be a haunted house. Before this house was built, the property that would become The Farm was part of a deed of land owned by Roger Williams. After he had been unceremoniously relieved of his position in the Massachusetts Bay colony, Williams made his way south to start a new colony that was named Rhode Island and Providence Plantations in 1636. Providence Plantations was the very first European American colony that would later become the state of Rhode Island after the American Revolution in 1776. Roger Williams and others wanted to colonize land with greater religious freedoms. The parcel of land that consisted of the farm was about 1000 acres in 1680 when the Richardson family, who had followed Williams, was deeded. Many of the 1000 acres have been sold off over time and now consist of 8 acres today.

The farmhouse was built in 1736 by the Richardson family, who had many hopes for the farm. Although many families had lived and died in the house, it is forever known as the Arnold Estate amongst the town folks. Over the centuries, many families have come and gone, each leaving a little bit of themselves within the walls of this home.

Perhaps, there were minute indications along the way about the secrets this house was compiling. Parts of the secrets would soon leak out when a family with five girls moved into the farmhouse in the 1970s. Slowly, the paranormal activity began, and soon they were under psychic acts.

Feeling panic and fear for the safety of the children, the beleaguered family contacted local paranormal investigators, who in turn contacted world-renowned paranormal couple Ed and Lorraine Warren.

The Warrens set about trying to eradicate the spirits in the home. At this point, there are various scenarios as to what happened in this home during the Warrens visit. The Warrens, along with a priest, did what they could to clear the house of any unwanted entities. The family continued to live in the house until the 1980s when it was sold.

(Above) The Farm

Not much is known about the haunting end of The Farm during these times as the new owners remained tight lipped regarding any activity. There were only a few mentions, here and there, of apparitions being seen by children in the home, and noises being heard occasionally, but not an awful lot. Coincidentally, John did a television show on the paranormal where they visited the farm which aired in September 2005.

At the time of the airing, there was a significant amount of activity in the home, but again, nothing came of this. This house might have faded into the background of haunted houses - that is until July of 2013 when Warner Brothers released "The Conjuring." It portrayed a cinematic tale about the family who experienced the paranormal activity during the Warrens visit back in the '70s. Suddenly, the farmhouse was catapulted into one of the most intense places on the planet.

The owners at the time, having had enough of all the hype - and still claiming that there were no ghosts in the house - sought to sell The Farm. Long time ghost hunter, Cory Heinzen, and his wife, Jennifer, found a chance to own a part of paranormal history at a price too good to pass up. So, in June of 2019, the couple purchased The Farm.

Cory and Jennifer have been close friends of John Zaffis, as well as the Elwards, for several years. Eager to show off their new home, they invited the three for a visit and investigation shortly after they moved in.

All three were eager to tour this home because of the paranormal notoriety, as well as the historical aspect. So, on a hot day in July, the three made the short trip to see the Heinzen's new home.

Driving up to the home, Debbie became increasingly filled with no small amount of trepidation about going to the house. "You know guys," she voiced to John and Larry, "For some reason, I'd much rather be riding a horse than be going to this house!"

John, always the investigator, said, "Why? This is a great opportunity for us. Just think of it. We are the first ones to investigate the Conjuring House since the 1970s when Ed and Lorraine did it. To my knowledge, no one has done an investigation in there since. And besides, it's been a while since we have seen Cory and Jen."

Larry, always the quiet one, just nodded, his mind wondering what sort of paranormal goings on they might encounter.

Suddenly, as they rounded the bend, there was the house. It seemed to beckon to the three in a false sense of welcoming as they drove the winding driveway to the house. There, at the door, Cory and Jen awaited their guests.

Entering the house is like stepping back into a gentler time when life was simpler but not necessarily easier. The house is decorated in eighteenth century furnishings, from the furniture and the candle chandeliers, to the hand stencils on the walls. All things aside, it is a lovely home that seems to grab ahold of you the instant you cross that mid-century threshold. But even with all this charm, there was something that lurked in the shadows out of eyesight, waiting and watching.

Walking through the house, Debbie began to feel energy swirling around her, trying to encapsulate her as she made her way deeper into the interior of the home. Shadow people peeked around old wooden door frames as the group walked by.

As they made their way to the front parlor, just off the birthing room that was now a library; the energy was on a high level. Debbie could hear many voices coming from all corners of the room. In the outer room that held a massive beehive oven, which at one time was the heart of the home, which was now cold and unused, she saw three children dressed in period dress. They were looking forlornly out the window, as if they were waiting for some loved one to return from a long-ago errand.

John asked, "Does anyone else hear someone crying?" He got up from where he was sitting and looked out the front windows, "I also saw someone. It looked like a woman heading to the front door."

The group heard footsteps overhead as the door to the laundry room swung open violently. A little startled Jen said "That door is hard to open, and it always sticks! It's never done that before!"

(Above) the beehive oven

(Above) The front door where banshee was seen

Cory went into the kitchen and found all the cabinet doors opened. He came back in and said "Every one of the cabinet doors is opened. We never heard a thing!"

John said "Do you hear that? The crying is back, but it is more of a wailing now! Similar to that of a banshee!" What disturbed the group was that the banshee is a harbinger of death. The group fell silent saying a quick prayer for their loved ones safety.

Shortly after all activity lessened and ceased all together. John and the Elwards made plans to come back. On the way home, they had a few psychic attacks. The three experienced headaches all at the exact time, and the car started to make weird noises, but as soon as they crossed the state line, all activity ceased.

For Debbie and Larry, the next day, July 4th, was a quiet day at home. Debbie was watching TV and decided to watch the movie "The Conjuring". Hey...why not, right? Suddenly, she heard someone call out her name from the kitchen. She got up from the couch, but no one was there! Was this the houses calling card?

Things got busy for John and the Elwards, as well as for Jen and Cory, who had recently opened the house for overnight ghost hunts. It was more than a year before they would return to The Farm.

In August of 2020, John got a call about doing a live streaming séance from the house on October 30th, some 47 years since the Warrens conducted a séance to find out what was in that place. It was the hope that some 47 years later that another séance might actually unlock some of the secrets of the house. Unfortunately, October is a remarkably busy month for John to do lectures at various colleges, so he was unable to join them, but the Elwards were available very excited about the prospect of attending the séance.

On October 30th, a freak October snowstorm blanketed the New England states, making travel difficult, but not impossible, for the Elwards to travel from their home to Round Top Road. Much of the technical staff had arrived as the Elwards pulled into the driveway. The show's star, Nick Groff, formerly of "Ghost Adventures" fame, was busy on camera, warming up the audience for the much-anticipated live séance. Larry and Debbie were ushered on camera to the basement area where they found Nick.

Nick was intrigued with the basement area, where there is a supposedly a grave within its stone wall. While standing there on camera, Debbie kept feeling an energy coming from the wall behind her, incidentally just about where they believed a body was interned. As she was describing the feeling to Nick, she heard a man's voice saying angrily, "Woman, woman, woman." She instantly felt that she was being admonished for speaking out of turn, as in centuries past women and children many times were supposed to be seen and not heard. She managed to say to Nick "I get the feeling that this house has many secrets!"

(Above) The Elwards with Nick Groff in the basement

Shortly thereafter was a report from one of the camera people that a large black mass was seen coming out from the well area. Many people have also reported an uneasy feeling associated with that area. Debbie,

Larry and Nick were no exception as she was the first to report that her legs were shaking, with Larry and Nick complained of sudden headaches. Stepping away from that area, the headaches were quickly dispelled as was Debbie's leg shaking.

After a short break, everyone convened into the living room where a large round table was being prepared for everyone to sit around for the séance. The séance itself would be conducted by an "eclectic witch," that is to say, a witch who selects what appears to be best in various doctrines, methods or styles. She incorporated into the table setting things from water, earth, fire and air - the four elements. The tabletop was sprinkled abundantly with salt, which for many people have a protective quality about it. Again too, it might have been incorporated as one of the elements. A small vessel was set in the middle of the table, and as smoke slowly seeped from this vessel, she added what appeared to be sage to it.

(Above) the séance

Soon people began to make their way into the room and to take a seat around the massive table. Everyone was instructed to place their hands on the tables. The witch began her chanting as she called on the spirits of the house to come forth and make their presence known. The smoke from the vessel rose slowly and seemed to circle in the same direction as the spirits were circling. A low growl was heard coming from the table. Participants witnessed shadow people peeking around door jams in the library, and knocking and footfalls were heard coming from overhead. The chandelier began to swing in the direction of the smoke. People experienced being touched, and spirits were seen looking in from the outside windows. Suddenly, the table gave a groan, as if the wood were cracking, and indeed the crack in the center began to split open, first a little at a time, then more and more as the séance continued. One young man became severely affected so the séance had to stop while he was being attended to. All in all, it was truly a night to remember. The house divulged none of its secrets, and it was felt that there is still much to figure out and to learn.

Soon, Nick and his film crew departed , but a few remained to continue the investigation. People were still experiencing paranormal events, but they mostly seemed to have died down.

Debbie and Larry planned to stay overnight with a few others. Turning in around 1 am, all seemed quiet and the house seemed to have settled down. A few hours later, Debbie woke up, shaking from a cold that seemed to penetrate her bones. She knew it was not from the cold night. Rather, it was a psychic cold. She could hear Larry gentling snoring next to her, but there were no other sounds. She did not venture to open her eyes, but she did feel as if she were being watched.

From somewhere in the house, she heard a soft noise. Then, she heard the grandfather clock chiming from below, doom, doom, doom, doom, but it did not continue, rather, gave a loud boom and no more. She fell asleep and did not wake up until the morning sun was streaming in through the bedroom window.

The smell of freshly brewed coffee and bacon drifted up the stairs. Life seemed to have returned to the house, and people started showing up for breakfast. Cory, the host, asked how everyone slept. Debbie said. "The only thing that woke me up was a "psychic cold," and then I heard the grandfather clock chime."

Cory said, "Come with me." She followed him into the other room and there was the grandfather clock. Cory said, "If you look, the clock has no workings. It's just the dial and the cabinet, nothing in there to make it chime."

Debbie looked and said, "I know what I heard."

Once again, the house held onto its secrets. As Debbie and Larry reluctantly said their goodbyes to Cory and Jen and to the house, they knew they would be back to see if they could uncover more secrets from the Farm on Round Top Road.

AUTHOR'S UPDATE:

Because of the pandemic, John and the Elwards have not gotten back to the Farm. Cory and Jen report things are still highly active. Since things are opening up once again, they are certain that they will return to the Farm in the not too distant future.

(Above) Reverend Larry, Debbie and Nick Groff

THE HAUNTED TOWN

By first accounts, Peninsula Bay, Michigan, looks just like any other ordinary town in the state. But as you cross the Stevenson Bridge into this quaint town, you first realize that there is something about this town that is out of the ordinary.

Johnson's General Store, just past the bridge, looks like it might have materialized out of a John Steinbeck novel. Locals still congregate there on a summer evening to sip root beer as the sun goes down.

Victorian era houses line the main thoroughfare to the Heaven's Gate cemetery, located on the west side of town. It is there that many of the towns founding fathers are buried and still seem to have a "say" in what goes on in local government.

One is immediately drawn to the quaintness of the town, but many visitors also are drawn there for another reason. As you drive across the Stevenson Bridge, you immediately feel an energy surge that is felt in most areas of the town. If you are lucky enough to be there after sundown, you may soon find out the cause of this energy.

A local couple, Candy and Sam Jones, contacted John late in the summer about anomalies that they were getting in their photos. They reported capturing many orbs of different colors while taking photographs throughout the town. Recently retired, their children had given Sam a new camera so that he would have something to do while enjoying his retirement. No one suspected that this camera would open a whole new world for the Joneses.

While taking photos around their quaint Victorian house, they noticed many orbs, some blue and some white, in many areas of the home. One place that was littered with orbs was a beautiful window seat area in their living room. The window was just one of the many beautiful ornate stained-glass windows which adorned the house. It looked out over the

148

side yard to the barn area. On either side of this window were two elaborate electric candles that, when lit, would give this area a beautiful, but eerie, glow.

At first Sam and Candy did not know why someone would build a window seat with electric candles on either side of the window. But upon research into the history of their house, they found out that this was the area that was used to lay out the deceased members of the family before burial. This would account for the lights and the stained-glass window. And this would also account for the many orbs that were photographed in this place.

Their large formal entry way was also an exceedingly popular place for orbs to congregate. John and the Elwards, upon visiting the Jones' house, felt that this was because of the many antiques that they had along the walls in this room. Sometimes antiques seem to hold psychic impressions associated with a former owner...much as a home would also have.

The barn on the Jones' property was also a terribly busy place for orbs. Here, Sam photographed many orbs zipping through the old horse stalls in the lower portion. An old garden area also seemed to be a hot bed of paranormal activity. The area outside the window that housed the window seat held a different kind of phenomena. There, Sam photographed what appeared to be a chain of orbs with a large hook on the end. This hook seemed to anchor itself against the wall of the patio, and the other end of the chain seemed to disappear into the house. Upon investigation of the area, there was nothing that could explain the anomaly in the picture.

But they were soon to find out that their property was not the only one that seemed to have orbs when photographed. The old mill that now housed the historical society also had many orbs that seemed to zip around the old mill wheel. Also, the Johnson General Store had its share of orbs as well as something else that Sam photographed that was very disturbing.

While taking pictures at the store, Sam snapped a picture of the side nearest the Stevenson Bridge. Once developed, he discovered a different type of anomaly in this picture. Instead of orbs, Sam captured a picture of a dark shadow that resembled a person's silhouette hanging from the nearby tree. The noose resembled the chain of orbs that they photographed on their property. They began to wonder if there was some connection to the hanging person and their property.

(Above) The chain of orbs

They researched their house some more and found that a man named Christianson built their house in the early 1900s, and from all accounts, it was the showcase of Peninsula Bay. Neighbors would watch as the many carpenters and architects labored to finish this show place. Mr. Christianson, who was an enormously proud man, wanted everything exactly right with his house. He, therefore, quite naturally, wanted a house that he could be proud of.

Upon completion of the house, the Christianson's held a gala party for the town's folk, many of them had never seen a house like this. The rich woodwork and flooring were beyond what their small houses had ever imagined. This house even boasted indoor plumbing, something that none of the other homes in the area had. It truly seemed that the small town of Peninsula Bay had come of age with the Christenson's new house.

Soon, many families from the area cities had bought land and made summer homes in this secluded area of Michigan. Although the town folk liked the money that the summer tourists brought in, they were very suspicious of anyone that did not grow up in their town. They became very "closed mouth" regarding any folklore in the area.

Sam and Candy found this out as they tried to find a reason for all the orbs in their pictures. Having not grown up in the town, they knew little about their home, and yet, no one seemed in a hurry to tell them anything about it.

John and the Elwards went there to see if they could find out anything. They were immediately assaulted with the psychic energy as they crossed the Stevenson Bridge, as well as many other areas of the town.

They had planned on researching the Heaven's Gate Cemetery on the west side of town, because on a recent walk, Sam had captured many orbs in its center. Upon investigation, Sam discovered many graves of the town's founding fathers.

While looking at the monuments, Sam heard a man's voice. He turned to see who had spoken and found no one. He looked in the direction of where the voice had come. He walked over to it, and the sensation of energy increased. As he got to where he could read the name on a gravestone in the dusky light of the setting sun, he was surprised to find that this was the grave of the man who had built the house that he and Candy were now living in. Here was the grave of Mr. Gerald Christianson.

Sam decided to go home and get a tape recorder and see what he could pick up, if anything, around the grave via EVP. He set the tape recorder on the monument and walked around, continuing to snap away on his camera. After a while, he picked up the recorder and hurried home to see if anything had been recorded.

Sam and Candy sat at the table listening to the play back of the tape. They could hear the summer insects and the occasional sound of the snap of a camera, but nothing else until almost at the very end of the tape. There was this strange sound of what could be described as wind and then a very gravelly sounding voice. As the voice spoke, it seemed to gather strength, and what it was saying became clearer and clearer. Soon, what it was saying repeatedly was "You come down with me!" Both of them immediately felt a cold chill envelope them as they sat in their warm kitchen. It was as if someone had turned on a large air conditioner.

John, Larry and Debbie arrived at Sam and Candy's house and made plans on investigating what they could in the town. As they drove over the bridge into town the energy was very apparent as was it in many of the areas that Sam and Candy had gotten the pictures. Later that evening, the three drove to the cemetery and waited to see what would happen.

They were so surprised to see many entities forming that night, almost as if they were eager to have someone to communicate with. They approached both John and Debbie and seemed to be communicating their messages.

Everyone that night could see and hear the entities. The grass was moist from the evening dew, and as one stood quietly still, they could hear footsteps approaching. And in the direction of those footsteps, you could see a form. This form was like those images that you see on a hot summer day as you drive along a stretch of road. It looks like there is water on the road, a mirage of sorts. Well, that's what these entities resembled. As they approached you, they seemed to shimmer in the dusky light like a mirage. As they got closer, details about them could be made out. The entities images seemed to blink and with each blink the detail became clearer and clearer.

That night, they were visited by a woman who was looking for a long-lost child, and a fireman who was trying to convey a message that he wanted someone to visit his grave, and another entity of an old woman who appeared to be lost and needed some direction as to where she should go.

Even though the true cause of these entities and the many orbs in the pictures have not yet been found out, it was an exciting place to investigate. Was the town actually a large portal? Why was it so paranormally active? John and the Elwards would like to go back next summer, where hopefully Sam and Candy will be able to break through the silence of the towns people and gain some insight as to what the cause of the many hauntings in this town might be.

AUTHOR'S UPDATE:

Sam and Candy have kept in touch with John, Larry and Debbie since their visit. They both have decided to move closer to their grown children. All though they will be leaving Peninsula Bay and their large home behind, Sam said that he will continue to take pictures, "Because you never know whom or what'll show up in them!"

PHELPS MANSION STRATFORD, CONNECTICUT

As the morning of March 10, 1850, dawned, it promised another cold and bleak day. The Reverend Eliakim Phelps was with his family, which consisted of his second wife and her three children from a previous marriage, and the couple's infant child. Reverend Phelps also had two grown children from his first marriage, but his wife died, and those children lived elsewhere.

The Phelps had purchased the grand mansion two years previous, and up until this day, had had no problems. That morning, the Phelps family departed from their house for a church service that was close to their home. Little did they expect the horror that awaited them on their return.

There was no indication as the family made their way down the winding path to their house. A surprised Reverend Phelps noticed that all the windows and doors in the house were wide-open, letting in the cold March air. The good Reverend was sure that the doors and windows were locked tight when the family left earlier that morning. As perplexing as the open windows and door were, they paled in comparison to the sight that greeted the family as they entered into the foyer.

It seemed like something out of a nightmare to the puzzled family. In one of the rooms, they found a statue like image of a person that was made out of their own clothes. At first glance, Reverend Phelps was shocked, thinking he had found the intruder. Throughout the main floor China dishes cups saucers and glasses were broken and thrown about. Mixed in was food and garbage. On the second floor, the family found their clothes ripped from the closets. Mrs. Phelps nightgown lay on the bed. The arms of the gown were crossed over the chest as if it were a corpse laid out for viewing. In each of the other bedrooms similar things were found.

Reverend Phelps told his wife to take the children back to church for the afternoon prayer service, and he would stay back at the house, hoping to catch the perpetrator if and when he came back. All though the Reverend tried in vain, he could not catch the intruder.

When he was upstairs, he would hear a commotion downstairs, and no matter how fast he ran, he could not see the perpetrator. And while he was downstairs, he would hear a commotion upstairs. Soon all became quiet, and Reverend Phelps crept downstairs.

According to Phelps, when he entered into the dining room, he was shocked to see eleven women in various forms of worship. Some were kneeling, and some were holding bibles. Upon closer inspection of these women, he found that they were stuffed statues made from the family's clothes. This went on and on well into the night with the whole family sleeping in one room.

There were many theories about the cause, and a few in town felt it was the kids causing it. They felt that perhaps the kids were upset over the new baby, and some even felt that perhaps the older Phelps children had come back in the house and caused their father all this trouble. It was felt that the older children resented their stepmom and that's why they were doing it. Others suggested poltergeist activity centering around Mrs. Phelps sons. Some town people even said it was the vengeful spirit of Goody Basset, who was hung as a witch not far from the Phelps house. But whatever the cause the Phelps decided to winter in their home in Philadelphia where they were not bothered by any bizarre activity.

The next spring, they moved back, and all was quiet in the house. In fact, they went onto live another 8 years in that house without any more incidents. The Phelps sold the house to another family who lived in it for decades with no activity up until they sold it in 1940s to a woman who turned it into a rest home for the aged. That is when the activity began to start up again, and in the 1970s a fire broke out and partially destroyed the house. It stayed vacant for a while.

John Zaffis, being an inquisitive teenager as well as a Stratford resident, had heard about the rumored activity in the old house from his uncle Ed and was curious. So, he and two friends went there to see if they could experience anything. Being young and impressionable, everything spooked them.

As they were going up the massive staircase to the second floor, they heard a loud clang that came from somewhere in the upstairs of the abandoned house. It sounded like a metal pot was being dropped. The boys knew nothing was left in the building that could have made that sound, so they both ran out of there as fast as they could never to return. A short time later, the house was bull dozed over, and nothing was left. A few years later, developers built new houses where once the grand house stood.

AUTHOR'S UPDATE:

It has never been reported if anyone in the new housing development built on the land where the grand Phelps mansion once stood ever had any experiences or any paranormal activity. John is now a bit older…. and a bit braver!

THE ABANDONED TOWN OF CONNECTICUT

In the early 1700s, three brothers founded a settlement atop a large hill in a certain area of Connecticut. The land was to be used primarily for farming, although the land was not particularly suitable. Many families joined the three, and soon the area was named after them.

But the settlement seemed to have been doomed to failure from the very beginning. As rumor had it, the young brothers' great-grandfather had been a nobleman in the court of one of the English kings. Despite his high rank at court, he had been accused and convicted of treason and then executed. It was also rumored that a curse had been placed on all the ancestors for the grandfather's indiscretions, and thus the legend of the curse was born.

Many people believe that the town's hard times and strange occurrences were actually due to the curse. Events surrounding the village became stranger and stranger. One of the first inhabitant's, besides the brothers, was a man and his wife. One day, a violent storm suddenly descended upon the village and a bolt of lightning struck the man's wife. The man was out of town on business and eventually returned. According to the townsfolk, upon hearing of his wife's death, he promptly went insane.

Over the years, stranger occurrences happened to the villagers. An epidemic struck the town, killing an entire family. Another strange occurrence happened when a local politician lost his bid for public office. It seems that a week later, his wife, who had been born and raised in this town, inexplicably took her own life.

In 1892 only one family remained living in the cursed town, and the wife died under mysterious circumstances. A few weeks after her death, their two little children disappeared, never to be seen again. And just a short week later, the homestead burned to the ground, and the poor beleaguered man, who apparently had had enough, walked away from the town never to return.

Over the remaining years, the village fell into disrepair, and no one ever lived there again. The word had gotten out about the "cursed" village, and no one dared to try, but that did not stop the curious from going there to see the village and to walk its streets.

The abandoned town is no longer open to the public and is now private property. Trespassers will be arrested, fined and have their cars impounded. But before it became private, John and the Elwards took a trip there to see for themselves what the rumors were all about.

The very first thing you notice is that it is so eerily quiet. There are no sounds of animals or birds. What little sound one may hear seems to be muffled. The houses are overgrown and only foundations remain. It is hard to imagine what the village may have looked like in its heyday. While walking down the pathways of the town, one is struck with the feeling of being watched. Dark shadows dart in and out of one's line of vision. In one foundation, Debbie sensed an old woman that was kept in the cellar hole when she was alive.

Muffled whispers could be heard in many areas of the old town. Photographs that were taken by the three would come out fuzzy and out of focus as if something did not want a record of their existence. The feeling of being watched was overwhelming, and a lot of curious visitors left quickly because of it. John and the Elwards did not stay long either as the constant feeling of being watched, along with the dark shadows darting around, gave them a very uneasy feeling.

AUTHOR'S UPDATE:

Because this area has been designated as a private land trust, the three have not ventured back to the village. They frequently hear accounts of people who have breached the borders without being arrested. They report that there is still a menacing feeling, as well as the eerie quietness. Whether this town was cursed or if all the strange happenings were just a string of unfortunate coincidences may never be known. But it would be wise not to try and venture there, as they have now increased security and they will arrest.

BOOTHE PARK STRATFORD CONNECTICUT

Our last haunted locale just might be our strangest: Boothe Memorial Park in Stratford, Connecticut. In 1914, two brothers, David and Stephen Boothe, created a memorial museum that housed twenty architecturally unique buildings. The brothers would acquire these buildings and transport them to their property and reconstruct them there.

The buildings include an old barn that dates back to the 1800s, a clock tower from Massachusetts, dating from 1913. And then there is the miniature light house, a trolley station, an old chapel from 1844 and a sunken rock garden with a rock podium. The Boothe homestead sits on the very foundation of a house that was originally built in 1663 that has been continuously occupied, although it has been remodeled many times over the years.

Of course, with so many different types of structures, each more than likely holding onto long ago energy, you would expect to hear stories about possible paranormal activity. Boothe Park does not disappoint.

During the late 1980s, a group about 15 people met regularly trying to contact any spirits. Many spirits were discerned, and some people believed that they were the spirits of Stephen and David Boothe. Many reported hearing rapping's, banging and a telephone ringing in the distance, but there was no working telephone at that time. It is believed that many of the family members are active only to protect their beloved home. There is a room in the home that is dedicated to the Civil War. Since it opened, there have been many reports of strange vibrations being felt. There have also been reports where people have picked up a feeling of sadness and oppression in the area.

Many people, young and old alike, have reported feeling chills in that room even on a hot day, as there is no central air conditioning in the house. There is a report of an elderly female visitor fainting upon entering the room. And still others have walked into this room, and for no apparent reason, turned around and walked right back out. Because of these strange occurrences, the officials have a chair by the Civil War room, ready just in case it is needed. But the Civil War room is not the only room in the homestead that has paranormal activity. The staff have felt strange sensations throughout the home. There have been sightings of a ghostly woman walking from the empty bedroom that was once occupied by Mrs. Boothe.

Being a sensitive, Debbie, upon visiting the Boothe homestead, had picked up on vibrations coming from all over, especially in the area of the stone podium. John, at one time, had taken a photo of an old coffee pot levitating off the stove.

AUTHOR'S UPDATE:

After many years of not being inside of the old homestead, John and the Elwards decided to take a trip to Boothe Park and made a walk-through of the home. During that trip many spirits were felt and seen in the home as well as other places in the park. It is felt that Boothe Park is still a very active place.

THE HAUNTED THEATRE

In 1955, on land that was once part of the notorious Phelps Mansion, the American Shakespeare Theatre was opened. The theatre offered the American interpretations of many of Shakespeare's plays, as well as the works of many other playwrights. The structure was patterned after Shakespeare's original Globe Theatre in London, England, which had been built in 1599. Over the years many famous and almost famous actors and directors tired their hands at performing and directing various productions. Some of the more notable actors were Katherine Hepburn, Will Geer, Fred Gwynne and Margret Hamilton of the Wizard of Oz fame, to name a few. In the first few years the playhouse was directed by John Houseman, of "Citizen Kane" fame.

In 1989 the Theatre held its last play, "The Tempest," and despite numerous fund-raising efforts for improvements and maintenance in order to remain an active theatre, the American Shakespeare Theatre closed its doors for good.

John and the Elwards had investigated the theater once and were witnesses to a lot of paranormal activity. Around the main entrance, there were many shadows that were seen moving about. Were these perhaps the ghosts of long-ago patrons still milling about...and possibly the actresses and actors who had once graced that splendid stage?

Walking deeper into the property, the three heard a distinct ladies voice that seemed to be reciting her lines of some play. Even though it was a warm summer evening, the air was cooler in this area. Debbie sensed a grandly costumed actress entering onto the stage. She made her way to the center of the stage and just vanished into a wisp. They also witnessed a glorious light show in the empty seats. Were these the memories of long-ago patrons?

They ended the evening as the activity began to die away.

AUTHOR'S UPDATE:

Unfortunately, in the early morning hours of January 2019, a massive fire ravaged and eventually destroyed the theater, bringing the hope of resurrecting the theater to a close. There were plans to still hold outdoor festivals, but because of the pandemic, the plans had to be put on hold. It is pretty much up in the air as to what will happen with the property.

LIZZIE BORDEN TOOK AN AXE

Who hasn't heard the old rhyme of "Lizzie Borden took an axe gave her mother forty whacks, and when she saw what she had done, she gave her father forty-one?" Or did she?

The highlight of any paranormal enthusiast is to spend a night at the infamous Lizzie Borden house in Fall River, Massachusetts. It was there on August 4th, 1892, Abby and Andrew Borden were brutally bludgeoned to death in their quaint two-story home on 92 Second Street in the textile town of Fall River, Massachusetts.

There were many speculations then, as now, as to who might have committed such a heinous act in broad daylight. Soon, speculation turned to Andrews's youngest daughter, Lisabeth, or Lizzie as she was called. The young woman was arrested on August 11, 1892, seven days after her parents were found murdered in her home. A week's long investigation was finally capped off with her arrest. At the time of her arrest, women were still thought of as being the weaker sex, and the news of her arrest was a sensation at that time. As Lizzie was lead to her jail cell, throngs of people lined the street, all clamoring to catch a glimpse of the young woman.

Lizzie's trial, arguably the world's first "Trial of the Century," began on June 5, 1893, to a packed courtroom and concluded on June 20, 1893. The jury deliberated for an hour and a half, returning with the verdict of not guilty. Many hours of evidence had been entered in the court records of the time. Lizzie went onto continue living in Fall River despite being ostracized by many who believe that she had literally gotten away with murder. She purchased a house not too far from 92 Second Street that she named Maple Croft and lived there with her sister, Emma, until an argument caused Emma to move from the house, never to speak with her sister again.

Lizzie continued to live there until her death on June 1, 1927, at the age of 66 of pneumonia. Nine days later, her sister, Emma, who had lived in a nursing home in New Hampshire, passed away at the age of 76. The sisters, who had never married, were buried, side by side, in the family plot in Oak Grove Cemetery in Fall River.

Over the years, many people have visited the Borden house as it was turned into a bed and breakfast. Some visitors are curious to see if they could get some insight into who could have possibly killed the Borden couple so long ago. A visit to the home is high on the list of "must do's" for any avid ghost hunter, and John and the Elwards were no exception. They were quick to accept an invitation when the opportunity arose. Although not as a team, all three have visited the house on Second Street and have had many encounters with the spirits that reside there.

Debbie had visited there late in the 90's. She remembers her tour vividly. It began in the front hallway where there was a mannequin that had a dress that was worn by Elizabeth Montgomery when she portrayed Lizzie in the movie "The Legend of Lizzie Borden."

The group was then led into the living room where Andrew Borden had been murdered and then into the dining room where the autopsies of the victims had been performed on the dining room table, and finally into the kitchen. The group was assembled in the front hall where they made their way up the stairs to the second level. After ascending the stairs, the group paused to look straight ahead to the John Morse bedroom, or the Murder Room, as it has become known, where the neighbors had seen the lifeless body of Abby Borden who was found between the bed and a dresser. It was thought that the murderer had snuck up behind Abby as she was making the bed and bludgeoned her to death.

Debbie looked straight ahead and saw what, at first, she thought to be a mannequin that had been placed their as an attempt for a "recreation." The woman ahead of her turned and looked at Debbie and said, " I find this terribly distasteful, especially with young kids on the tour. And I am going to say something!" And with that the woman made her way to the tour guide to voice her displeasure.

The tour guide looked at the woman and said, "I am sorry, but we don't have a mannequin in that room the only one we have is in the front parlor."

Debbie looked again and the floor in the murder room was clear. Whatever she and the woman had seen was gone. Nothing was there but the carpeted floor.

Another time that Debbie and Larry visited the house, they spent the night along with a few other ghost hunters. Larry, although usually affected by the spirit energy, felt it at once. He became so tired that he laid down hoping to regain some of his energy. He later decided to forgo the séance.

In the murder room, a psychic was brought in to do a table tipping experiment. Debbie was eager to join in as the psychic began by calling in any spirits that might be lingering in the house. They all held hands as the table began to slowly vibrate and move. Slowly, the table began to rise, and at first, it fell back to the floor. But soon, it rose to a few inches, and then began to wobble and pitch back and forth.

Spirit energy swirled around the room. Many people reported hearing whispers and voices as the table tipping continued. Finally, the table fell back, and all activity stopped. Everyone that had participated in the table tipping ritual was exhausted and soon all retired to their rooms.

Debbie laid down next to her snoring husband on the bed that had once belonged to Abby and Andrew Borden and soon fell asleep. A noise from the depths of the house awakened her around 3 am. All seemed quiet, but as she swung her legs over the side of the bed, she heard a man say, "She's awake." Then all was quiet again.

She made her way downstairs and found a small group assembled in the cellar. There were many reports of a lot of paranormal activity in that area, as well. Debbie felt a male spirit push past her as if he were fleeing from something a long time ago. Is it possible that this male spirit had something to do with the murders and now was stuck in a proverbial prison where he was designed to live the tragic event over and over each night? Unfortunately, his name and identity has been lost to history but that does not stop his plight.

John also has been to the house many times over the years. He has also had his share of experiences with the supernatural in the home. One particular memorable encounter happened to him as he spent the night in the attic room. He had retired for the night and found that he tossed and turned all night long with crazy dreams. Even though he didn't remember specific details, they were all bizarre in nature. In the morning, he got up and headed to the shower and found three large bruises on his back that looked like someone had punched him. Not waiting for breakfast, he left right away.

AUTHOR'S UPDATE:

Over the years John had become good friends with the owner of the house, but unfortunately, she passed way in early 2021.

HAUNTED OBJECTS

Photo by Dan LeRoy Productions, LLC | danleroyproductions.com

As many readers are aware, John has a large collection of haunted objects that he keeps in an adjacent building on his property. There are many items that were given to him by former clients that were relived to get the cursed thing out of their homes. Housed in the building is a collection of dolls. Now for some reason many people fear dolls. Perhaps because it is the likeness to a person or maybe it's their staring blank eyes that unnerves many a person. Whatever it is, John continually receives many dolls from all over, and often with just a note that says simply "TAKE THIS PLEASE!"

Also in his collection are items that have seemingly taken control of their former owner's lives and thus making them a hell on earth. Many times, the former owners did not know exactly what was going on until it was almost too late. Then, they would contact John, who would travel to help them and remove the items. Here are a few of the many items that have found their way into John's museum to be kept safe from causing harm to others.

THE FAMILY PHOTO ALBUM

The invention of the camera made it easy to keep pictures to remember a family member or special event. Photo albums to keep the photos in became popular and soon became a show case in the Victorian home.

Around 1850, photo albums began to become popular, and a Victorian woman who was knowledgeable with arts and crafts, soon found a way to take the plain paper and make intricate designs, giving an extra bit of artistic flare to the photos. There are many fine examples that have survived to this day and can be seen online.

As the camera improved, many photographers would go door-to-door or town-to-town in search of customers who wanted to capture their fond memories and preserve them in an album for all to see. Many times, a person sitting for the picture would not actually be alive.

After having passed, many families would commission a photographer to visit in order take photos of their deceased loved ones, or as they were known at the time, as "memorial portraiture" or "mourning portraits." This rather macabre practice might seem a bit odd in this day and age, but to the Victorian age it was the only way that a loved one, many times a child, could be remembered.

Over the years John has received many objects, ranging from the hideous to the beautiful. Some are everyday items that have taken on an "otherworldly" presence and have wreaked havoc with some one's life.

One morning in late May, John received a package in the mail, and inside he found an exceptionally beautiful photo album. It seemed to be made out of a heavy carpet like material. It was very ornate and most likely had at one time taken center stage on a coffee table.

(Above) The postmortem photo

The person sending the package wrote to John, "I picked up this ornate photo album at the local flea market. I liked it because it was so unusual - the colors and the texture and all. But soon after coming home with this, things began to happen around my house. Cabinet doors would be opened when I got up in the morning. and I would hear the sound of doors being slammed, but no doors were touched.

(Above) Victorian picture album

"Other things began to happen too. I began to have nightmares of a young girl dressed as if she were coming from the Victorian era. At that point I had never looked at the album, having gotten busy and a little distressed over what was going on in my house. But that afternoon I sat down and began to thumb through the photos, and there were many pictures of serious looking men and woman and some of children, as well.

"I came to one picture, and well, it did not look natural to me. The young woman looked like she was dead. I had heard that many times there were pictures of the deceased taken for remembrance purposes, and I felt that this was the case of this young woman, and it scared me because the girl in that picture looked just like the one in my dreams, so I am immediately sending to you. Please call me if you have any questions."

John called the woman to inform her that he had received the package containing the album. She was glad he called and told him that since sending out the album she no longer has nightmares of Victorian Age people nor any paranormal problems in her home.

AUTHOR'S UPDATE:

Anyone that has seen the album remarks that there is an energy to it, either because of all the family photos or because of the postmortem photos. Perhaps it's a combination of both. John makes sure to keep it away from anyone who might touch it. Binding prayers have been recited over it and it is incased for safety.

VINTAGE HOMEMADE OUIJA

As is so often the case, a person with a haunted item does not want anything to do with it after having John speak with them. He often just receives the item with no explanation whatsoever as to what is going on. Usually, he will leave the item out in the sunshine to de-energize and purify the item before he can add it to his museum. Such was the case with this homemade Ouija board.

John had never seen anything like it before. It is made on a piece of burlap and is about 18 inches by 18 inches. There on the first line is capital letters from A to G in block style lettering. There are two letter As, Cs, and Es all the rest are single letters. On the next line that have the letters H to O, only the letters L and N are doubled. On the next line, which begins with the letter O, a double from the previous line, the only letter doubled is S, and the line finishes with Z .

The next line there is TAK a space then MIE, then below that the numbers 0 to 9. The burlap material possesses an extraordinarily strong odor of incense about it. There are no marks or areas of wear as one would expect to find if a planchette was used, so John thinks maybe a pendulum was used as a way of communicating or a wine glass. The board does give off a remarkably high level of energy. Many who have come in contact with the board have reported a sick feeling of nausea,

The sender did not give any information except that this was old and that they tried to bind the spirit but to no avail. They did put the item in a box in an outdoor shed and noticed immediately that things were better, which is why they sent it to John.

(Above) The homemade Ouija board

AUTHOR'S UPDATE:

John has tried unsuccessfully to contact the sender but has heard nothing back. He can only surmise that all is well or else he feels that they would have contacted him.

GRANDMA'S CRYSTAL BALL

Many times, people do not necessarily know what their family members are really into. A lot of time, things are hidden, and family members are shocked when the truth comes out. Such was the next case when John was contacted by a granddaughter who upon cleaning out her grandma's house came across a rather strange item, something she had never imagined her grandmother was into.

The granddaughter explained to John, "To me, my granny seemed like the perfect stereotypical grandma. She always had cookies, freshly baked from the oven, whenever when we came to visit and little presents for each of us. Well, granny got really sick and went downhill fast, and she passed a little over a month ago. And the task of cleaning out her house went to me, because I was the only family member she had left.

"Granny did not keep much. There were the usual birthday cards, announcements and stuff like that, but way back in her closet I found two Items. They were sort of pushed back into a corner of the closet. John, it was a crystal ball!"

He asked, "Was your grandma a practitioner of the divining arts?"

The granddaughter continued, " I didn't think so at first, but I began to think back to when I was little and when granny had 'visitors' and I had to play outside while the 'visitors' were there. They always stayed only about a half an hour. So, I really do not know. But wait! I found something else. It was a book on palmistry with strange notations and people's names next to dates. I do not know what to make of it. But that is not the strangest as I brought the two items to my house and almost immediately things began to happen."

John interrupted, "Tell me what is going on."

(Above) Crystal ball

The granddaughter said, "I heard my name being called, and the funny thing was, it sounded just like granny. I almost wrote it off as a vivid imagination, but the next morning I woke up and all my living room and kitchen furniture was flipped over. I never heard a thing, and all the refrigerator contents were strewn about the room. I have never had this happen before I brought the ball and the book home. John, I boxed them up this morning and am sending them to you. Please let me know when you receive them."

He said he would, and few days later, a box arrived. Upon opening it, he saw that it was the book and the crystal ball. Carefully, he removed the items after grounding and protecting himself. He placed the crystal ball on a table and the book next to it. Right away, the crystal ball seemed fog over with what looked like clouds beginning to swirl around the inside of the ball. He immediately placed the ball in a specially designed container that he uses for such items. He placed the book in there as well. He then transferred the container to the room where he houses all his new acquisitions until they can be placed safely in his museum.

AUTHOR'S UPDATE:

John made a call to the granddaughter, and he was happy to hear that once the items were removed from her house all was quiet.

THE UNMASKING

Masks have a multitude of uses, ranging from a sanitary use as a medical professional would use, on Halloween to disguise oneself or even for nefarious uses like illegal activity. Another common usage would include ceremonies of some sort, maybe religious or celebratory. There are people who collect masks for as many reasons as there are uses for masks. Jason Morgan was one of these people.

Born and raised in Alaska, he had spent his formative years surrounded by the beauty of the Inuit people of his area. He had always marveled in the beauty of the many artifacts of these people. He had always held such artifacts in high regard and had always treated them with the respect that they deserved.

A few years previously, a dear friend, who was also a collector of Inuit art, had passed away and had left Jason one of his most treasured masks. This mask was a rather large round one made of wood, and it almost gave the impression of a moon or sun. Curious, Jason read the paperwork that had accompanied the mask. "This mask is from the Inuit people who are the descendants of what anthropologists call the Thule people, who emerged from western Alaska around 1000 AD. This mask was used primarily during the summer equinox as a celebratory item to ensure that their crops would flourish during the upcoming summer months. "

Jason filed the paperwork away and hung the mask in the center of his other masks. A few days later, he came home from work to find that all of his masks, with the exception of the new one, were lying face down on the floor. Puzzled, he didn't think too much of what could have happened. A no-nonsense person, he simply picked up each mask and hung them back up and continued his evening without giving much importance to what had happened.

(Above) Intuit mask

The next night, he came home and, once again, found all the masks scattered around the floor. Also, once again, they were face down with only one mask left hanging...the new one.

This time Jason began to wonder what was going on. He figured that if the masks fell due to a vibration, then all the masks would have been on the floor, including the newer mask. This time, he hung the masks up and made sure that all were hung securely. Despite being a no-nonsense type of person, he still had been brought up listening to the legends and myths of the locals, so he was not ready to rule out anything without a little research on his own.

He also setup a camera in the hopes that he might catch the action that was causing the masks to fall. After making sure that all his equipment was running, he left for work. And again, when he came home, all the masks were found face down on the floor. Eager to find out why, he rewound the tape and what he saw certainly made a believer out of him.

At first, nothing out of the ordinary showed up on his video, but about halfway through, he saw a large shadow rise up in front of the masks. This huge shadow figure raised its hands, and all the masks except the new mask fell to the floor, face down. Then, the shadow seemed to bend forward as if it was bowing to the mask, and then it disappeared as quickly as it came.

Shaking, Jason called a friend that was into paranormal happenings, and had him come over and see the video and help him to deal with what was going on. Jason's friend, Ted, was excited and concerned for his friend.

Jason asked, "What should I do? I don't feel comfortable with this mask in my house anymore."

"Well," Ted said, "I know a man who lives in Connecticut that will take this and place it in his museum to keep it safe so no one will come in contact with what might be in or around this mask." Jason was eager to get in contact with Ted's friend. Ted said "His name is John Zaffis and he's a real down to earth type of guy. I know he will help you with this."

John had just sat down at his desk to answer some emails when his phone rang. Noticing that it was an Alaskan number, he curiously answered the phone, "Hello John Zaffis."

On the other end Jason, a little surprised as to John having picked up the phone right away, began "Mr. Zaffis, my friend Ted told me to call you. I have this mask that I believe is haunted and I need someone to take it and keep it safe from others coming into contact with it."

John answered, "Well first of all, tell me what is going on and why you believe the mask is haunted?"

Jason began, "Well a few weeks ago, my good friend, who was a collector in Inuit art, passed away. He left me one of his ceremonial masks that was given to him by from the Inuit people from Alaska. I am a collector as well but do not have as many as my friend did.

"Anyhow, I hung the mask on the wall, along with my other masks, and each day I would come home and find all my masks on the floor face down. That mask was not touched. I am not a believer, or should I say I was not a believer in the paranormal, but I placed a camera on the wall where the masks were when I went to work. I honestly thought it might be a joke or prank, and I wanted to catch the person doing this.

"I came home that night and, once again, the masks were on the floor, but that mask was still hanging there. I rewound the video, and I could not believe what I was seeing. The masks just came off the wall, one by one, onto the floor, face down. There was also this large shadow that materialized as the masks came down, and it seemed to almost bow to the mask left hanging, the shadow just disappeared.

"I just want this mask out of my house. I just don't want to take a chance in anything else happening. I have heard too much local lore to take a chance on this."

"Well," John said, "If you really want to get rid of the mask, you may send it to me, and I will make sure that it placed in my museum so that it will not come in contact with anyone." This is what Jason was hoping for. He thanked John and promised to send out the mask the next day.

A few days later, John was just turning into his driveway when a delivery vehicle pulled up behind him.

Said the driver, "Mr. Zaffis, I have a package for you."

Taking the package, John noticed the postmark was from Alaska, so he knew it was the mask that Jason had sent him. John opened the package outside. He always opens the packages he receives outside in the sunshine; this light is a pure aspect of nature and is very beneficial energy that helps to bind any negative energy. Only after this step does he place the item in another area of the museum where he can have prayers and blessings done over them and only after that is done does he place the item in the museum.

As John opened the package, he immediately noticed that it was a very large mask, and that it resembled a face which seemed to draw you into its empty eyes. Around the "face" of the mask, there appeared to be markings that looked like the rays from the sun or moon. On top there seemed to be some sort of ornament. He was not sure what this mask could have been used for, but he felt that it was of significant importance. He hung it in a prominent place in his museum where it has been hanging there since he received it.

AUTHOR'S UPDATE:

Shortly after receiving the mask from Jason, John heard from the young man. He told John that he had researched and found out that the mask was a Shaman's Sun Spirit mask. It was purported to be a very powerful mask and was used during the summer solstice ceremony. A large amount of respect, homage and honor would have been given to this mask, as use of this mask was vital to ensure that the tribe's crops would flourish thorough out the summer growing season. Jason also reported that all was quiet in his home that no more of his masks were falling from the walls. And he is very glad to rid his home of that mask.

MISCELLANEOUS

Photo by Dan LeRoy Productions, LLC | danleroyproductions.com

THE SKINWALKER

This next case was a first for John, Larry and Debbie. Here they would encounter an ancient entity...a Skinwalker. According to Native American legend, Skinwalkers are shape shifting witches and are a powerful and destructive presence in a tribe. These witches are reported to have the abilities to transform into animals. They are reputed to be able to "possess" people, and it is also said that they can bring people back from the dead. They wear animal skins and skulls, hence the name Skinwalker. They are feared amongst their people, although they live openly amongst them, they are not talked about for fear of vengeance. Some researchers theorize that they are beings from another dimension.

John had just finished his morning coffee when the phone rang. Taking a final sip of the liquid gold, (John is "diehard" coffee lover), he picked up the phone. A very distraught woman named Susan was contacting him in hopes that something could be done to help her and her husband, Jim.

John, after trying to calm her, asked "Susan can you fill me in a little as to what's going on at your home?"

Susan began, "There seems to be so much, I don't know where to begin. I guess I'll start with when Jim and I moved into this home about five years ago. It was ideal. Everything was perfect! A beautiful river runs behind our house, and Jim loves to fish, so he was thrilled to have that. There is a beautiful field across the street that is at the foot of a mountain. You can see deer grazing almost year-round.

John told her, "That sounds lovely, but could you talk about when things changed and what activity is going on, please?"

Susan said, "Oh I'm sorry! I am just so nervous, and I never thought I would have to call someone about this. I guess it started just around the time our renter up and left. She gave us no notice, nothing! She just up and left in the middle of the night! That is about the time that Jim was fishing one morning when a tall man approached him and told him he could no longer fish there as it was private Indian property. Neither Jim nor I knew this. Right after this happened, strange things began to occur around the house."

She paused, and John said "Ok...now what kinds of things are happening?"

Susan was almost reluctant to tell but, hesitantly, she started. "We've seen shadows, heard knockings and banging. Things have gone missing, our names have been called, we've been touched, and just this morning my husband woke up in our front yard naked, with no memory of how he got there!"

John interrupted, "Is your husband prone to sleep walking?"

Susan answered that he was not and that "his pajamas were found outside torn to shreds as if some wild animal had ripped them off, but he did not have a scratch on him!"

John told Susan that he and his crew would investigate her house and see what they could do. He called Debbie and Larry and asked them to join him, sure that Debbie's psychic ability would help in determining what was going on in Susan and Jim's house, and that he would be needing Larry to bless the house at the very least. John always like to be prepared, just in case.

It was a few hours' drive to Susan and Jim's upstate New York home. The sun was beginning to set as they pulled into the driveway, but as they got out of the car they were taken back by the beauty of property. It was everything that Susan had said and more. The setting sun illuminated the mountain in a rich vibrant purple color, giving it an almost mystical appearance. In the background, the sounds of a river could be heard as the three watched a herd of deer move slowly over the field. It was almost picture perfect, but still there was something that lay hidden, something waiting for its cue to show itself on center stage.

Susan and Jim met them at the front door as they walked up the cobblestone path. Both were middle aged and had looks of trepidation on their faces as they ushered the three into their small living room. As they sat down with Susan and Jim, John wanted to start immediately, so he began asking if they could do a preliminary walk through. John likes to have Debbie walk through the areas that the client claims are active. She and John began with the bedroom. There she picked up on some negative energy, especially on Jim's side of the room.

She walked through the kitchen and living room and then outside to the front yard. It was there she noticed that the energy level began to rise. She followed it out into the field where the negative energy continued to increase. Almost seeming to be perplexed, she stopped short of the woods "Something doesn't feel right in this spot," she said.

Looking at the ground, she observed footprints. Tentatively, she and John followed the footprints. They wound through the trees and up an incline where there was an outcropping of rocks. One of the rocks had a wolf's head carved into it. As they walked passed this rock the footprints turned to into paw prints.

As John and Debbie looked at one another, both heard a loud growl. John yelled, "Let's get the hell out of here!" The woods seemed to take on a life of their own as they quickly made their way back to the safety of the house.

Black shadows appeared all around them as they crossed the field. They heard the sound of a large animal thrashing through the undergrowth, but they didn't stop to see what it was. Breathlessly, they made it to the safety of the yard, and only then did they turn to look back. The woods once again looked normal...no black shadows, no sound of an animal thrashing about and no growling.

John and Debbie walked through the large backyard. There, they had an unobstructed view of the river and of the road leading to the Indian reservation. They both noticed a person walking in the distance. He seemed tall and straight as he ambled along. Just as he got level with where they were standing, he stopped, bent down, and appeared to morph into a four-legged being. This creature continued walking on all fours and then morphed back into a human-like figure standing upright again on its two feet. It looked back at Debbie and John and vanished. But just as it vanished it cried out: "Yee naaldlooshii!"

Later John had this translated into English and it means "It goes on all fours."' John thought to himself: "Well, this just became a different kind of a case."

Once back inside the house, John filled the others in on what had happened. He felt that the Skinwalker might have thought that Jim and Susan were desecrating Indian land by being there. Perhaps it was the spirit one of the deceased elders of the tribe who did not like Jim fishing in the river. Maybe this was somehow an affront to the Native Americans. He felt that they may never know the exact reason or reasons for all of this activity because Skinwalkers were usually associated with the Navajo tribes. This was Connecticut after all.

Because of his many years in the paranormal, John knows and works with clergy from all denominations. So, he made a call to a local Native American shaman with whom he had worked with before. The shaman agreed to come out immediately and see what he could do. This was particularly exciting for Larry and Debbie. Larry enjoys observing and working with clergy from other denominations and faith traditions and Debbie has some Native American heritage.

John first had Larry bless Susan and Jim and the inside of the house. Then the shaman took over the outside areas, quieting down the land and the woods. Because of the darkness, John, Larry and Debbie could not see what he was doing but opted to respect his privacy as he walked into the woods.

He made offerings to the Great Spirit to ask forgiveness for anything that might have transpired there that was taken as a sign of white men desecration. The ritual and prayers went quietly. There were no outward manifestations of any spirits. There was only the smell of burning sage as it slowly wafted towards the house, carried by a soft breeze. Whatever spirits were there were hopefully being appeased by the shamanic ritual and ceremony. The shaman, John and the Elwards left with the promise to keep in touch.

AUTHOR'S UPDATE:

Jim and Susan have kept in touch with John, and they report all is quiet in their home. After some research, they discovered that their property had once been a "medicine camp" or "pow wow" camp. This is a sacred area where a shaman would attempt to cast out evil spirits from the afflicted tribe members. Many times, these camps would be near a body of water. Just to be on the safe side, however, Jim no longer fishes in the river. There have been no more shadows and no more Skinwalker sightings. Once again life is good for them.

A WARNING

Due to their work in the paranormal field, John and the Elwards are ever vigilant to any strange occurrences in their lives due to a case that they may be working on at the time. Sometimes, things occur even before they get involved with a case. For example, Debbie will many times receive strong psychic feelings or premonitions in the form of clairvoyance about things as either a warning or as clarification.

One of these premonitions occurred while the three were driving to a case in New York. A good-natured bantering began between them, something that happens a lot when the three got together.

John jokingly said to Debbie, "If you're so good, what color is this house we are going to?"

Debbie looked at him and said, "It's a salmon-colored house with a white picket fence in front and two large flowerpots by the front door." Sure enough, they soon arrived at their case, and the house was indeed salmon colored, complete with a white picket fence, and at the front door, there were that two large stone urns with flowers. None of them had been to this house or had seen pictures of it either.

A lot of similar warnings happen to Debbie because of her abilities. She will get strange smells, touches, or see visions involving the upcoming case. She may also have dreams about the case, even before she even knows what it is all about. It is kind of like an early warning system, so to speak.

They have been doing the work for many years, and the devil has tried his little tricks to get them angry at each other. He tries to lose things on them and to try and make their life unpleasant. But through their faith and their genuine desire to help people, they have persevered where many have faltered. But the three always wonder what the "dark forces" have in store for them. They have found that the answer to "what its next move is" in this cosmic chess match between good and evil. It can be almost anything.

Both John and Larry, too, have experienced these so called "notifications" from the spirit realm just before a case. But none of these warnings have been severe enough to cause the three to take extra precautions. They, for the most part, had been "ghostly" in nature, nothing more than a knock, a touch or missing items. These were just annoying little occurrences to alert them of an approaching case. That is until this occurrence happened.

Larry, Debbie and John also have ordinary jobs that they do when they are not doing paranormal investigations or eradicating spirits from people lives. One such day, Larry and Debbie had been at their job working with children at their local YMCA.

As they arrived home, they noticed nothing out of the ordinary as they drove to the front of their apartment building, but as they opened their door, they immediately smelled smoke in their kitchen. At first, it was not an alarming thing as their landlady's son smoked, and they figured that he had been visiting his mother in her downstairs apartment. But as they walked further into their apartment, the smell of smoke was more prevalent.

They both ran around looking for the cause. Debbie went into the den and found that Larry's altar was terribly burned. The hob nail candle sticks were completely melted and unrecognizable. The candles were gone. His pewter chalice had a huge hole in it, as if some metal piercing missile had been fired through it. The paten that holds the Holy Eucharist was melted over the top of the chalice. Antique altar linen that was on the top of the altar was destroyed. The top and front were charred and there was a small burnt line that went up the wall from the top of the altar in the back. But the amazing thing was that most of the holy items on the altar were not damaged, almost as if the fire went around them.

(Above) Chalice and patten

(Above) Top left of altar

Larry had a relic of the true cross that was kept in a large wooden cross on his altar. This was not touched. It was even scorched. It looked as if the fire was diverted around it by some unseen protective barrier. His mass book was also untouched, as was the area surrounding it.

(Above) Top right of altar

There was a small icon of Jesus and Mary that was charred at the corners, but was mostly left untouched, as well as the pyx, a small container that holds consecrated hosts. Also on the altar was a relic of the veil of the Blessed Virgin Mary. The back of the metal reliquary still had charred linen from the altar cloths attached to it where the fire had burned around it. They pulled off the linen and found that the relic was intact. There were just a few scorch marks on the back between the metallic reliquary and the linen that was left on it. Also, the wooden stand that the relic usually stands on was not touched...the fire once again looked as if it had been miraculously diverted around it.

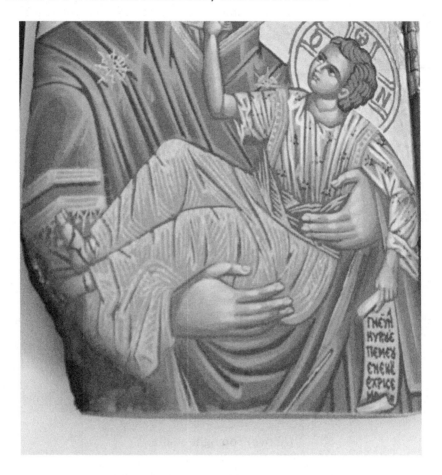

(Above) The icon with the burnt edges

The altar, which was a converted dresser, had a drawer which was charred by the fire, but none of the religious books or missals he kept inside were touched.

What had caused such a bizarre fire? There could be many possibilities. Larry could have left the candles burning, but the candles would have been burned out near the bottom. And could candles left burning have generated enough heat to turn hob nail candle holders to liquid so they could melt? Could this kind of fire also melt pewter as it did with the paten or generate enough heat to burn a hole through one side of a pewter chalice and out the other side? It should be noted here that pewter begins to soften at 471 F (244 C) and becomes fully molten at around 563 F. So that fire had to be extremely hot, but it did relatively little damage.

And how can you explain the damage to some areas, but not to other areas, as well as no damage to anything surrounding the altar, except for the small fire damage to the wall. There were very combustible things on either side of the altar that were not touched. It was as if the altar was the fire's prime goal.

You can find an explanation for the fire, like leaving the candles burning, that could have ignited the linen, but can you find an explanation as to why some things were destroyed, like the candle sticks, the chalice and the linen. But why didn't the wooden cross, the relics, the wooden stand or the religious books burn? If the fire was hot enough to melt glass and pewter, then with all logic, the whole room should have gone up in flames.

John, Larry and Debbie feel that this was once again an attempt by the evil realm to try and destroy their work, and that once again, Divine protection was sent their way. They continue to do the work and will continue to be on the alert to anything the devil might send their way.

John, too, has had his share of unexplained events around him, as well. One time, John was driving to a case not too far from his home. His car began acting up, barely making it up the hills. He feared he was going to break down at any moment. Somehow, he made it to the house, but was astonished that, what was only a forty-five-minute drive, had taken him over twice as long. He met a priest there who was doing the house blessing and he mentioned the trouble he had had on the way there. The priest offered to say a blessing on the car which John agreed to. On the way home the car gave him no more trouble and the homeward bound trip took less than forty minutes.

AUTHOR'S UPDATE

Although the Devil still tries to throw roadblocks in John, Larry and Debbie's way to stop them from helping people under paranormal attack, they continue to take it all in stride and muster on.

Larry's altar, along with the chalice, paten and a small glass orb (which is all that is left of the hob nail candlesticks) are now safely housed in John's paranormal museum.

John took his car into the service station, and they found nothing wrong with it, the mechanic felt it was probably a "clogged fuel filte,r" in which the clog had worked its way free. He has had no more problems with the car since.

The three continue to be ever vigilant to what the demonic might do next.

THE WENDIGO

A Wendigo is a mythological creature, or perhaps an evil spirit, that the First Nation Algonquian tribes who have their roots at the border of Canada, Nova Scotia and along the Great Lake Region believe in. According to Native American legend, this creature is said to inhabit these regions of the north. They are believed to be born during the cold snowy winter where travel is limited and food is scarce. The creature grows over this time and their appetite becomes insatiable, therefore, in a few tribes is referred to as the creature "Born of ice." When the spring thaw begins, these creatures, also according to legend, begin to roam looking for a host or victim.

A few lucky ones have encountered one of these creatures and managed to escape its cannibalistic ways, meaning this being feeds off its intended victim's soul rather than eating the person's flesh. These lucky souls describe the creatures as unnaturally tall, gaunt with grayish complexion and withered skin that seems to cling to its bones. It is said that it resembles and smells like a freshly disinterred corpse.

Only a powerful shaman can get rid of these demonic creatures, because they are the only ones who are knowledgeable and powerful enough to be able to outsmart the tricks and wiles of the Wendigo.

If you know John Zaffis, you know that he has a museum of haunted artifacts. His museum has objects that range from a statue of the Virgin Mary, whose hands were melted off during an exorcism of a house and the family that lived there, to a life size mannequin wearing the ritual wear of a notorious witch. Mingled amongst these many diabolical items, John likes to mix harmless items as a theme. But please note that his most "dangerous" items are kept separate from the other less volatile items. They are kept in special containers sealed with special binding prayers and exorcised salt. Because of this, John as well as the Elwards, are always on the lookout for items that would accompany any one of his many themed rooms.

John happened upon one of these themed items at, of all places, his in-law's house. "Momma Mary," as John affectionately called his mother-in law, was sitting in her chair as John and his wife, Cheryl, walked into the house. Mary had a large box in front of her on the floor, and she reached into it and retrieved an item all wrapped in paper. Slowly she began to unwrap the item, just as John and Cheryl entered the room.

"What do you have there, Momma Mary?" John asked.

"Let me show you!" she answered. From the box, she pulled two items that she had already unwrapped. She showed them to John and Cheryl as she finished unwrapping the third. "I saw these three dolls in a store, and I fell in love with them."

John looked at each doll and said to Mary, "Oh I'd love to have these, not that they are haunted or anything, but I'd like to put them in my Native American themed display."

Mary looked at him and said, "When I'm gone you may have them."

John said, "You know...they remind me of the shaman I met when I was up north, when the Elwards and I encountered a Wendigo."

"A Wendigo?" Mary said. "Please tell me more."

John said, "Well, sit back and I'll tell you all about it."

John began, "A few years back, the Elwards and I were in the Great Lakes region doing a case at a home near one of the Indian reservations of the area. Some of the activity that the homeowner was claiming were noises that seemed to be coming from the walls. And yes, they checked for mice. They had observed shadows that resembled some really grotesque human shapes, foul smells and scratches on various family members. There were some young kids involved, so we got there as soon as we could. But we were not the only ones that would be going in to help the family. Because of the proximity to the Indian reservation, a local shaman had also offered his services, as well. We were meeting with the shaman before we were to go to the client's home. He would be filling us in on what he would be doing as well as learning what we would be doing."

John continued, "There was a local Native American lore regarding a Wendigo. Many of the tribal members believed that one had been unleashed from its lair on the reservation to the nearby homes when some of the contractors building the homes had accidentally disturbed a pile of sacred stones that the tribe believed held the Wendigo at bay."

John paused and then continued, "The shaman and the tribe believed that Wendigo was the problem in this house and the shaman also felt there were other entities that possibly were 'helping' the Wendigo torture this family. Boy," John continued, "this had the makings of quite a case!"

John stopped and took a sip of his coffee, seemingly lost in thought as he continued. "So anyway, the shaman explained many of the rituals he would be performing, but he cautioned us that there were some that were very sacred and only reserved to a member of the tribe. He requested that we allow him to do these rituals alone. We agreed to his request and made our way to the house."

Again, John paused to take a sip of coffee, in the meantime Cheryl and her father had sat down to listen to the story. John then continued, "To see the house from the outside, you would never in a million years think that there were problems. It looked like any other house in middle class America. But once you crossed over the threshold, you suddenly felt like you were thrust into the bowels of hell itself! You were first assaulted by the smell, which was like a mixture of feces and sulfur. On top of the smell there was a feeling of dread, as if at any moment the other shoe would drop. There were a myriad of noises emanating from the air, in all rooms.

"In the living room, as the family ushered us in, suddenly there erupted a scream. It began as human-like, but reached a crescendo of that of a wild animal that had just been eviscerated by some beast. We all jumped

199

and looked around half expecting to see some horrific scene that would correlate with the sound that we had just heard!

"Next from somewhere on the second floor, a noise began slowly, sounding like some sort of a methodical pounding that appeared to resonate within the walls, floor and ceiling. It started slowly, then became louder and louder until we felt our ear drums might rupture. And then, just as suddenly as it started, everything stopped!

"The man of the house turned and looked at us and said, 'This happens all the time every day, this is what our life has become!' I will tell you this family which consisted of a husband, wife and three kids: two boys and a girl. They all looked beleaguered by the constant onslaughts of this entity.

"The woman then turned and looked at us and said, 'We have no place to go or to send our kids to! We have to huddle together for safety and somehow survive this nightmare!'"

Momma Mary looked at John with tears in her eyes, "How horrible for this family! I can't imagine trying to live through something like that!"

John nodded and continued, "I can't imagine it either, but somehow families that go through these things summon a strength that gets them through it until help can arrive. Ok well, where was I? Oh yeah...as the sounds died down and the smell started to dissipate, things became eerily quiet, as if the entity was trying to figure us out.

"I asked the couple if we could do a psychic walk through of their house. I still needed to get a feel for what was going on, even though the entity had shown its true colors the minute we crossed into the house. I wanted to make sure there was not something hidden that we might miss. So, Debbie, the shaman and I went to tour the house, while Larry sat and talked with the family.

Considering the magnitude of what was going on in the home, it was clean and orderly. Lots of times when a family is going through a paranormal problem the houses are usually in disarray, but this house was as neat as a pin.

"This puzzled me at first until the shaman saw my questioning looks and said, 'The Wendigo does not destroy property, just lives. It wants to use the victim as a host so that it can eventually kill it. Much like a cat, it plays with its prey until it tires of the game and then it will kill it. Time is of the essence as we do not know as to the timetable of this creature. I think it's best to begin as soon as possible'.

"I agreed with him, and we joined the others. The shaman began to get ready, as did Larry. Both priest and shaman took out their tools of their trade. The shaman took out a sweet grass bundle, salt, an abalone shell and a feather, while the priest took out his ritual book, salt, and holy water. Both men endeavored to not leave any stone unturned in their joint effort to eliminate this entity.

When everything was ready, the shaman began to speak in his native dialect, spreading his arms wide and facing the stairs to the upper level. The shaman said in a loud voice 'ch'jjdii ha'go wa'shde'e' alyaii ye-an-zen no danihinihi!' which he later told us loosely meant 'Demon comes here. The creator wants you!'

"He repeated this twice, when suddenly the house seemed to creak and groan, and it felt like it was shuddering. From somewhere upstairs came the sound of thunderous footsteps that shook everyone and everything in the house as if there was an earthquake happening. The footsteps came closer to the top of the stairs. They became more and more thunderous, causing things to vibrate. Soon we all began to lose our balance, that is, except for the two holy men.

"Larry had begun reciting his prayers from his ritual book as the shaman commanded the wendigo to come forth. Suddenly, at the top of the stairs, we could see this large black mass forming. It slowly came down the stairs one step at a time. With each step, the black mass began to take on a shape. Slowly, it began to resemble a creature with had a large humpback on his left side. Its arms hung loosely at its sides. It had a barrel chest and skin that resembled the skin of a reptile. But the face was something directly out of a nightmare. The head was large, somewhat disproportionate to its body, and there was a large horn on the top of its head that resembled the horn from a rhinoceros. The thing had four sets of ears and a broad flat forehead. Its eyes were small yellowish slits under two heavy black eyebrows. The nose was long, like that of a horse. At the end its nostrils was a large opening that was oozing and dripping into its mouth. It had a mouth that resembled the mouth of a hyena but with several rows of razor-sharp teeth. It had a long tail that split in two that kept thrashing around the more the prayers from both men. It legs were short and stubby. Its knees resembled a camel's knees, and it had two large frog-like feet. All in all, it was a formidable beast, and it looked really angry at having been summoned." John paused once again taking the last sip of his coffee.

He noticed that his audience was hanging on every word he said. Finally, Momma Mary said, "Well...don't keep us in suspense. Tell us what happened! Did you help the family?"

John nodded his head and said, "I'll tell you...for a while thing were tough, and we seemed to be getting nowhere, but Larry and the shaman kept praying, and slowly the wendigo seemed to be getting weaker and weaker. It had not moved from its spot on the stairs, so whether it was afraid of coming closer or if it did not have the strength or power, we will never know. For soon, the entity let out a howl that ended up as a death like gasp and it just slowly disappeared, until it was gone all together.

"The shaman had Larry finish up his prayers throughout the house, and then he asked us all to step outside while he did his private ritual. This was to ensure that the demon would stay gone. Once completed, he met everyone outside and wanted to bless the land with tobacco, salt and arrowheads as an offering to appease any spirits that might have shown up. And just like that, it was over and done with, and the shaman left.

We went back in the house, and things felt exceptionally light. There was a hint of the smell of sweet grass in the rooms, but all was quiet. We left shortly afterwards, heading for home once again."

John got up to leave, but Momma Mary stopped him and asked, "Have you heard anything from the shaman or the family since your visit?"

John said, "About six months ago, I heard from the shaman. He saw the family recently, and they reported to him all was well. The house was quiet with no more strange smells, noises or shadows. Thankfully, peace and quiet has returned to their home."

Momma Mary smiled and looked at the three dolls in the box and said, "I am sure these dolls have a story that they are anxious to tell." Momma Mary smiled once again and would say no more.

(Above) Momma Mary's dolls

CONCLUSION

Now that you have finished reading "When Spirits Speak...We Listen," we hope you have gained some insight into the various aspects of a paranormal investigation and the different ways in dealing with them.

It should be noted that not all entities leave as quickly and benignly as in these cases. Many will seek revenge on us for what they feel is an interference on our part with what they are attempting to do in the clients life. Many times, there are countless hours invested by us in a case to bring it to a conclusion. The cases that you have just read about have been condensed and highlighted to save the reader the boring or mundane aspects of the case. If this were not done then it might read like this: John and the Elwards walked into Gloria's living room where her seven-year-old cat was lying asleep in the corner of the sofa. Gloria noted to her guests that she had rescued "Precious " from the local shelter and had spent a good month before "Precious" would come out from under her bed, and a good fifteen-minute narrative on "Precious" then would follow. These mundane facts have been left out of the stories and just the important activity has been recorded in this narrative to draw the reader's interest.

Also, it was decided to give the reader a quick lesson on the paranormal in hopes of helping the newbie investigator in determining what they might be up against when dealing with a case. By all means, we are not suggesting that you follow what we do. It is rather just a suggestion on what you may encounter, like we did, and how we dealt with it as a guide.

ABOUT THE AUTHORS

Most people know John Zaffis from his various television shows, including *The Haunted Collector*. A respected demonologist, John has spent over four decades researching and investigating the paranormal.

Debbie Elward is a talented psychic medium and a researcher. She's able to walk through areas with ghostly activity and pull information from the ghostly inhabitants, providing the team with more information regarding the haunting.

Reverend Larry Elward is an independent priest who uses his faith and prayers to deliver closure to haunted locations. He not only assists souls in crossing over into the light, he is also a seasoned exorcist.

Using their unique talents, the three are able to walk into haunted locations, identify the haunting and then rectify the situation, bringing peace to both the living and the dead.

For more information, please visit John Zaffis' website: JohnZaffis.com

Made in the USA
Las Vegas, NV
23 December 2023

83490396R00125